What I Want My Adopted Child to Know

An Adoptive Parent's Perspective

Sally Bacchetta

iUniverse, Inc.
New York   Bloomington

What I Want My Adopted Child to Know
An Adoptive Parent's Perspective

The views expressed in this work are solely those of the author and do not necessarily reflect the views of the publisher, and the publisher hereby disclaims any responsibility for them.

iUniverse books may be ordered through booksellers or by contacting:

iUniverse
1663 Liberty Drive
Bloomington, IN 47403
www.iuniverse.com
1-800-Authors (1-800-288-4677)

Because of the dynamic nature of the Internet, any Web addresses or links contained in this book may have changed since publication and may no longer be valid.

ISBN: 978-1-4401-9436-8 (sc)
ISBN: 978-1-4401-9438-2 (dj)
ISBN: 978-1-4401-9437-5 (ebk)

Printed in the United States of America

Library of Congress Control Number: 2009912368

iUniverse rev. date: 2/24/2010

For Erin and Ryan
I love you bigger than the sky

Contents

Acknowledgments

This book would not be in your hands right now if not for my husband, Dennis. It was he who convinced me I had something to say and he who refused to let me quit until I said it. Throughout the writing of this book I relied on him for perspective, encouragement, clarity, and balance, and he never once let me down. He is a rarity – a true partner in every sense of the word – and co-author of everything I am. I thank God every day for the husband and father Dennis is.

Adoption has brought many people into my life who might not otherwise be in it. Each of you is in this book, either by direct contribution or by changing who I am as a mother and a writer, and I am grateful to all of you for sharing yourselves with me. I owe particular thanks to Alaina, Amy, Angie, Ann, Britt & Barry, Bryn, Christine & Wayne, Doris, Dory, Erica, Gen, Heather, Jackie, Jessica, Jesse, Julie & Ron, Julie, Lauri, Leslie, Maggie, Marie, Mary, Nicole, Paula Jean, Robin, Sylvene & Jay, Tammie, and Tess for helping shape this book.

I am also especially grateful to:

My parents, Joyce and Fritz Snyder, for giving me my life. My siblings, Laurie Snyder, Michael Snyder, Holly Swantek, Jennifer Kerr, and Dan Snyder, and their spouses and children, for animating it.

Meghan and Jenessa, for your faith in me.

Jen, for making me a better wife, mother, and Christian.

Jill Mulcahy, for your insight, your honesty, and the depth of your loyalty and friendship.

Tabetha Ammon, for understanding everything and giving so much.

Dave Lytle, for believing there is no distance too great.

Greg Franklin, for your counsel and friendship.

Barb Monahan, Mary Walsh Snyder, Dawn Smith-Pliner, and everyone at Friends in Adoption, whose commitment to open, ethical adoption brought my family together.

Karen Rabish, LCSW-R, for your ongoing support.

Dr. Michael and Nurse Linda Martin, for your unwavering dedication and compassion.

Casey and Tim, for changing my life.

Patricia Irwin Johnston, whose unexpected generosity led me back to myself.

Ann Fessler and all the Girls Who Went Away, for your honesty.

Foreword

Adoption is nobody's first choice—not for any member of the "Adoption Triad." As a way to build a family, adoption is the choice most prospective adoptive parents make only after they have exhausted all of their biological options. Birth mothers don't plan an unplanned pregnancy, and they agonize over their adoption plan, sometimes choosing to parent instead. Adoptees have no say in the matter—the decision is made for them. Without consultation, adoption decisions are made out of love, sometimes out of desperation, and the person about whom all of the decisions are being made has had no voice.

We adoptive parents, and I am one, dance with our emotions, our dreams, our family and financial realities before making the decision to try to adopt a child. And, having made that decision, the really hard choices begin—which path to follow, which fears to discount? Every adoptive parent's story is unique, but the common themes are many—loss, grief, frustration, fear, impatience and confusion are eventually, hopefully, replaced with joy and discovery, and later the fears and confusion which come from actually being a parent! In the end, the trek towards adoption is motivated by one thing—to be parents. And there is no greater joy, no deeper anxiety, than that experienced by parents.

The adoption process is challenging, annoying, revelatory and unkind. It prepares us little to be parents, adoptive or otherwise.

It is a rite of passage, an entry into a club to which we would give anything not to belong. But it also gives us something in common with other adoptive parents, and a story to tell, advice and cautions to pass on to others following in our footsteps, joys to recount.

Sally has written a narrative which is heartfelt, honest and warm. She's told her story truthfully and without sugar coating, but also with knowledge from which I would have benefitted had the book been written before my family embarked upon our own journey to adoption. I can identify with Sally's story—I have seen it repeated over and over again—with my friends, with my clients, and my family. And we adoptive families have all traveled the same paths about which Sally has written so eloquently and emotionally.

I know that Sally and her daughter would not be a part of each other's lives, mother and daughter, without the disappointments and travails of adoption. I've seen Sally and her daughter together many times, and her daughter has the same sparkle in her eye as Sally, the same playful spirit, the same sense of humor. I don't know if these traits exist because of nature or nurture, fortuitous cosmic coincidence or just plain happenstance, or none of these. But it doesn't matter, because they are mother and daughter, however that happened to occur.

I am tremendously lucky. I'm lucky that adoption brought me my son, and that led to my decision to become an adoption attorney, and that led eventually to meeting and working with Sally and Dennis. I am lucky to have been able to be a part of their story, and the stories of so many other birth parents and adoptive parents. And Sally's children, and the readers of this book, are lucky to have the benefit of Sally's experience and her shared wisdom, because her story reminds us that we have so much in common.

Gregory A. Franklin, Esq.
Adoptive parent
Fellow of the American Academy of Adoption Attorneys

Introduction

Adoptive parents don't love their children the same way biological parents do. That's an uncomfortable notion for a lot of people, but it's true. We *don't* love our children the same way. We *can't*. That's not who our children are. Our children come to us from someone else. They were conceived without our knowledge or participation. They lived in someone else's body, and the most important decision about their lives was made by someone else. Our children carry someone else with them into our hearts, and we love them differently because of it. Never less, sometimes more, but always differently.

Adoptive families navigate emotional terrain that fully-biological families don't have to. As a young child I learned that babies are made in a special way between a man and a woman who love each other very much. Well, neither of my children was made that way. My husband and I have to figure out how to teach our children that sex is a sacred commitment between adults, knowing that some day they will realize they were conceived under very different circumstances. Biological parents don't wonder if their son's birth mother is still living with her abuser or using drugs or in jail; they don't have to formulate a response to "Are you going to give me away someday?" But neither do they have the anticipation of meeting birth parents, the joy of finding birth siblings, or the delicious irony of strangers saying "Your daughter looks just like you."

Nothing about parenting is simple. All parents juggle their dream, their instincts, and conventional wisdom, and in the end, most of us leap with faith. All parents know the challenge of letting their children struggle, the pain of watching their children hurt, the humility of falling short of their own expectations. What's different for adoptive parents is that adoption adds an undercurrent to the parent-child relationship, and every decision we make passes through that current. Everything we think, everything we say, everything we do is nuanced by adoption. When our toddlers act out, when our adolescents experiment with new identities, when our adult children reject us, we experience all of that against the backdrop of adoption. We analyze all of that within the context of what we know and don't know about our children's birth families, and we wonder about the long-term effects of adoption on our children. We wonder if we are enough.

Right now, our daughter is perfectly at peace about having grown in her birth mother's tummy until she was ready for us to bring her home. I'm not looking forward to the day she realizes that before we became her parents, her birth parents made the decision to place her for adoption. In the most basic sense, she was in fact rejected from one life before being accepted into another. That's a tough reality for a lot of adoptees. It's also a tough reality for a lot of adoptive parents. Being an adoptive parent is like having one answer for every five questions. The longer I parent the better I become at savoring the sweetness of the answers I do have and letting go of the questions that remain. I've learned to embrace the dizzying bounty that adoption brings to my family, and I can say with conviction that I wouldn't change a thing.

What I Want My Adopted Child to Know is a book adoptive parents can give to their child and say, 'I know adoption is painful, unsettling, joyous, and affirming. It's that way for me too. More than anything, adoption is the way we came together, and I'll always be grateful for that.'" Wherever you find yourself among the pages of this book, I hope that *What I Want My Adopted Child to Know* makes your life different, just as adoption does.

Sally Bacchetta

Chapter 1

I Would Do It All Again

When I look back over my shoulder at the path I took to adoption, I wonder how close I came to living a different life altogether. I wonder which of the roads not taken would have made all the difference. What if your father and I had met earlier than we did? What if we had gone further with ART (assisted reproductive technology)? Would I have biological children if I had given up caffeine? What about the meatless diet, the kickboxing, and the fall from a ceiling beam in the barn? Did any of that affect my ability to conceive?

I reflect on every fork and detour and I wonder: If I had been able to conceive and carry a child, would I have adopted you anyway? I'll never know, but I like to think so. I like to think we were destined to be together. I like to think that by God's plan or some cosmic choreography, all roads led to you. I like to think that no matter which direction I traveled, I would end up here. With you. There's no way to know for sure, and I guess it doesn't really matter anyway, because here we are, officially "us." And I would do it all again.

You know your birth story; I've told it to you many times. That is, I've given you what details I know of the who, the when, and the where of your coming into the world. I've also told you about our coming together. You know how happy I was the first time I held you. You know who was there and what everyone said. You've seen the first pictures of us together, and you know the story of your homecoming. But there's another chapter in your birth story, a chapter that's not so much about you. It's *my* chapter. You see, your birth story is also my birth story, because the mother I am was born when you were born. You made me a mother. You made me *your* mother. And for me, our birth story actually began long before you were born.

I don't know anyone who dreamed of growing up, getting married, and not being able to have children. I certainly didn't. I assumed that when (if) I decided to have children, one of my perfectly ripe eggs would let her guard down for the most athletic of a throng of swimming suitors, and I would simply get pregnant as women in my family have done for generations. I would have children the regular way, if I decided to have them at all.

I didn't think about adoption much, and when I did, it was as a really nice, slightly exotic thing to do. A really nice, slightly exotic thing for *other* people to do. Older couples who never had children, or people who wear sandals year-round and quit their jobs to become missionaries, or families who fix up old Victorian mansions and seem to collect assorted "children with special needs" or kids from "broken homes." Adoption was something those people did—not me. Why would I?

I peed on a forest worth of tiny test strips before I started to think that maybe "it" wasn't going to happen—not without some help, anyway. So I climbed into the stirrups. I consulted the experts. I filled the prescriptions and charted my temperature and scheduled sex. I stood on my head right afterward and tried not to cough or sneeze the rest of the day. I got X-rays of my insides and injections in my backside. All of my once-private entrances and exits were transversed, transmographed, radiographed,

2

photographed, sanitized, anesthetized, magnified, pulled and pried, palpated, saturated, dilated, inseminated, and evaluated in a series of attempts to get pregnant. And the harder I worked at it, the easier it seemed for *other* people to get pregnant.

Every time I turned around, I bumped into another swelling belly—my younger sister, my older sister, my sister-in-law, my friends, my neighbors, my coworkers, your father's coworkers, my hairdresser, the bank teller, stray cats—and except for the cats, they all paraded around like they medaled at some reproductive Olympics, like they had "Competent Uterus" or "Fully-Functioning Female" stamped on their foreheads.

It's not their fault they're fertile, I thought, so I forced my smile and offered congratulations. I gift-wrapped yet another Classic Pooh creeper from yet another baby registry ... and I hid in the closet with my empty uterus, crying so hard and so long I ran out of tears. I prayed for at least one viable egg and just a handful (is that really *too* much to ask?) of motile sperm, and for patience and grace and enough self-control that I didn't snap and smack the next bloat-bellied broad who chirped "I just love being pregnant!"

I worked my way dutifully—and with increasing panic—through a rigid curriculum of specula, specimens, pillows, and pills, approaching my pre-prenatal calisthenics with religious fervor—injection, collection, inspection, rejection. Begin again. Injection, collection, inspection, rejection. Begin again. Until the day I didn't begin again. I just couldn't. It wasn't anything I planned or even decided, really (unlike the hundred self-imposed deadlines I had deliberately blown right past, pretending not to notice that I was a year, or two or three, beyond the last line I had drawn in the sand. *If I'm not pregnant by the time I'm X age, I'm not going to try anymore. I don't want to be* that *mother*). One day I just stopped trying. Something happened inside me or nothing happened, I don't remember. I just stopped.

Some people move easily from the dream of having children to the dream of adopting them. They are more attached to the idea of raising children than they are to genealogy. Plan A didn't work; it's on to Plan B. No big deal. Others need time to grieve the losses of infertility before they can conceive of another way. Sadly, some people who want very much to adopt are weighed down by the prejudices of family members who think they can't bond beyond their bloodlines. And many of us never recognize our own quiet biases about adoption until it becomes intensely personal. That was me.

I was angry. I was petulant. I was wounded. I was painfully surprised to find that I was a snob. It turned out that deep within my most private self, without meaning to, and never overtly, I thought of adoption as a default, a less than. Apparently, I thought of adoption as a last resort for people who were out of options, people who had failed to produce their own children, people who couldn't make a family the regular way, people who were desperate or broken. People like me.

I didn't want to be people like me.

I resented having to consider adoption. I resented my body for betraying me. I resented being wired to want kids. I rejected the notion of having children that weren't *really* mine. I disparaged pregnant teenagers for doing in the backseat what I couldn't do in the sanctity of my marriage. I was angry at your father for bringing home a book about adoption, and I was barely civil to the cavalcade of social workers, attorneys, and adoption agency staff who traipsed in to invade my privacy and whose file folders on my kitchen table were tangible proof of my fundamental inadequacy. I despised my need for them even as I desperately wanted their help.

I cried and raged and judged and fumed and, after a long while, accepted. I accepted that things happen the way they happen. It is what it is. I accepted myself and my situation. I accepted that it wasn't really *my* situation at all; it was *ours*, your father's and mine. I accepted his perspective and his feelings and his help, and eventually, I realized that adoption is as natural for some people as pregnancy is for others. I accepted adoption as legitimate, as legitimate a way as any other of becoming a parent. Once I got my head and my heart around that, I began to embrace adoption as the right way for me to become a mother. I grew to cherish the idea and even feel special. Adoption emerged as something self-evident and fulfilling and romantic. I fell in love with the idea of adoption, and I began to bond with my child-to-be-adopted-later even before choosing an agency to work with.

I was ready to adopt long before I was ready to tell other people I wanted to adopt. To say it out loud made adoption a scarlet "A," proclaiming my deficiency to the world. I no longer thought of infertility as a failure, or adoption as a defeat, but I was convinced that other people did. To tell it to someone else was to confirm their whispered speculation and make myself an object of their pity. I didn't want or need anyone's condolence. I had made my peace with adoption, and once I fell in love with my child-to-be, I developed the same fiercely protective streak that most parents have. I was sure that even if they didn't say it, other people would think of my child as a less than, a settled for, a "better than nothing." The idea of adopting my child had become better than *anything* to me, and I couldn't bear for anyone to think less of her or him.

I thought that coming to terms with the idea of adoption would be the most difficult part of the process. Was I ever wrong! The time I spent deciding to adopt was a walk in the park compared to actually doing it. It turns out that adoption is a tremendous hassle. It's intrusive and time-consuming and expensive. Again and again we had to convince strangers that we were fit to parent, while every day brought another story of parents who left their babies alone in the car or served alcohol to underage teens.

We got fingerprinted and evaluated, looked over and passed up. We gave strangers access to our financial records and our bedroom closets, knowing full well that plenty of biological parents were cruising along with stale batteries in their smoke detectors, pot handles facing out, and wall outlets uncovered.

We spent over a year researching agencies, attending seminars and workshops, and filling out endless application forms. We talked to everyone we knew who had adopted. *Did you go private or public? How did you do your networking? If I may ask, what costs were involved? How long did you have to wait?* We became adoption experts, well-versed in private versus public, domestic versus international, open, closed, intrastate compacts; the Intercountry Adoption Act; and the Hague Convention. We learned the difference between surrender, relinquish, and termination of rights, and between adoption agencies and adoption facilitators. We deliberated about sibling groups, transracial adoption, and children with special needs. We compared the pros and cons of adopting domestically and from China, Russia, Guatemala, Chile, and the political climate of each.

We talked to parents who had adopted through foster care, some of whom thought it was right for them and others who admitted they wouldn't do it again. One adoptive-from-foster-care mother said, "There's no way to prepare for the heartbreak of loving children who can't or won't ever really love you back." I was daunted by the prospect of trying to heal children who are old enough to understand that they have been rejected or abandoned, and whose hearts and spirits are often quite bruised. I was haunted by visions of children who are unable to attach, who withdraw, self-abuse, or act out aggressively against the parents who have waited a long time to love them. I know that's not the case with all children adopted from foster care, but still I wondered if I was prepared to take that risk. *What kind of a person am I if I say no? Would I be the best choice for that child?*

Your father and I lay awake at night ruminating: *What do we want? What can we handle? What will our families support? Should we adopt domestically? What will our life be like when this baby is a school-age child? A teen? Are we in a position to immerse our child in a culture different from ours? Is ongoing contact with the birth family beneficial or confusing for the child?*

We learned to live among stacks of paperwork—background checks, medical exams, child abuse clearance forms, blood tests, bank statements, dossiers, letters of reference, our personal portfolio, each precious referral and potential lead. We had breakfast with the ICC report, studied the CAP book during lunch, and went to bed each night with more questions than answers.

Apparently, my inability to conceive implies a corollary potential inability to parent, at least to the people who can make or break an adoption. The first step toward proving our parental fitness was to complete a home study with an adoption social worker. Wanting to make a good impression, we bought carbon monoxide detectors and fireplace guards, we stuck Tot-Finder decals on the windows of your future nursery, and we even vacuumed behind the refrigerator. We cut the grass, washed the windows, put the coffee pot on, and reminded each other not to interrupt, tap our pens, laugh too loud, talk with food in our mouths, or swear. And for heaven's sake, agree with each other about everything!

The home study interview questions, and there are many, seem easy at first:

> What age child do you hope to adopt?
> Would you consider a sibling group?
> In what religion, if any, do you plan to raise your child?
> Will there be a stay-at-home parent?

As the interview goes on, the questions become more challenging:

> Are you open to a child of a different race?
> Would you consider a child whose birth mother had multiple sexual partners and whose birth father is unknown?

Are you open to a child who has spent two or more years in foster care?
Would you agree to visits with the birth mother three times a year?

And finally, downright uncomfortable:

Are you willing to accept a child born with one or more physical deformities?
Would you consider a child conceived through rape?
Would you consider a child conceived through incest?
Are you open to a child whose birth parents are mentally retarded?

As we answered "yes" or "no" to mental illness, history of attempted suicide, illegal drug use, alcoholism, cleft palate, asthma, cystic fibrosis, premature birth, smoking during pregnancy, dwarfism, exposure to HIV, I became more and more self-conscious. I felt violated, having to answer these questions while a social worker recorded our responses—a social worker whose impression of us mattered a great deal. The adoption process forced us to make public some of our most private biases and limitations, some of which we didn't even know we held.

We finally received word that our paperwork had been processed and we were officially "active" or certified for consideration. *Great news! OK, where's our baby/child/referral?* We waited and waited and waited for someone to call and say that a birth mother wanted to meet us. For a long while, I leaped every time the phone rang. *Maybe it's the agency! What if it's a birth mother? Has the baby been born yet? Is it a boy or a girl?* Day after day the phone rang and it wasn't the agency or a birth mother. Day after day the babies being born weren't for us, and one day I didn't leap for the phone. I just walked. And after more days and more babies who weren't ours, I didn't even walk, I plodded. Plodding eventually gave way to just staying on the couch screening phone calls through the answering machine.

The wait was absolutely agonizing. There were no OB/GYN appointments or baby showers to mark the time. No ultrasounds or heartbeats to suggest that our baby had in fact begun the journey to our arms. No one asked how I was feeling or if we'd chosen a name or "Hey, when's the big day?" When you're waiting to adopt, children don't ask adorable questions like "Did the baby crawl in there by himself, or did his daddy put him in?" or "Can the baby come out just for a minute so I can see it?" or "Doesn't it get tired of eating your mashed-up food?" Strangers don't offer unsolicited advice in the elevator or the checkout line or in public restrooms. As annoying and intrusive as strangers can be, I craved their interest as an affirmation that baby existed and parenthood was imminent. Adoption is like an invisible pregnancy, with nothing to suggest you're any closer to being a parent today than you were yesterday, or last week, or last month.

Not being a member of the pregnancy sisterhood, I missed out on all the prenatal pampering and impromptu parenting advice from veteran mothers. And many people, when we told them we were hoping to adopt, simply didn't know what to say, so they said less and less over time, and eventually we had only the occasional support group meeting or phone call from a social worker to reassure us that Everything Happens The Way It's Supposed To. *I was supposed to bear my own children. That's the way it was supposed to happen.*

When you decide to adopt, you open your heart to disappointments and near misses that bring you to your knees. A birth mother who calls every day for a month with prenatal updates suddenly stops calling, and out of respect for her hormones, you try to give her some space. But you can't eat and you can't sleep and you're out of your mind with anxiety, because you've already decided she's carrying your baby. Sure, you've heard of birth mothers changing their minds in the birthing suite, but that's not going to happen, because that's *your baby* she's carrying.

But really, it's not. Really, it's hers. It's her baby, her DNA, her body, her pregnancy, her labor, her delivery, her choice, and her baby belongs right where it is as much as any baby belongs to the womb that cradles it. Whatever prenatal bonding goes on happens between her and the baby. You're not a part of any of it, except in your own mind. Regardless of what's been said and written down and agreed to, regardless of how much you like her and she you, regardless of the freshly painted nursery, it's her baby until she decides otherwise. *If* she decides otherwise.

Even a few weeks after you bring the baby home, a birth mother may change her mind and decide to parent. Her parents may decide to parent their new grandchild, or her best friend may convince her that babies are always better off with their natural mothers. Or the baby's birth father, who has absolutely no intention of parenting, may refuse to terminate his parental rights, simply because he's pissed off at the birth mother for dumping him. It doesn't matter that you named the baby after your grandmother. It doesn't matter that you've taken 135 pictures of her sleeping. It doesn't matter that you've already forgotten what on earth you used to care about before she was born. She's not your baby. Not anymore.

You struggle to see through scorching tears to pack the diaper bag and find your keys. You gently snuggle a tiny skull cap onto a tinier head and slowly cinch the straps on the infant carrier. It feels every bit a nightmare as you kiss your precious love for the last time, and the (*We Know It's Very Painful … Hang In There*) social worker drives away with your baby. You stand there, rooted in the driveway. You're in shock. You're no longer a parent. Just like that.

You have lost your child. You have lost the child you waited years to find, and there's nothing you can do. There's no formal grieving protocol. There is no funeral or memorial service, no bereavement leave from your job, no sympathy cards to acknowledge your loss. Even though your pain is as potent as that of any parent who loses a child, most people don't understand that. It didn't happen to them, so they don't get it. Your family blames the System that allows children to be taken away from people who love them. Well-meaning friends criticize the birth parents—*She shouldn't have made an adoption plan if she wasn't sure. He doesn't really want the baby; he just wants to get back at her.* You graciously explain that you're sure the baby's birth mother loves her, and you're sure that if she is able to parent, it's in the child's best interest, and you're sure that things happen the way they should. But deep in your closet, you're only sure that your baby is gone and your heart is now as empty as your uterus.

Many times I inched to the very edge of conclusion. Many times I thought, *I'm done. I want out. This is costing me too much of myself.* I finally realized that in the moments when I was closest to surrender, I was also closest to peace, and that's when I knew I was ready for you. I knew then that I was ready to be your mother because I had let go of the way I wanted this to happen and opened up to whatever way it happened. I had released my ideal, I had chosen the reality of my motherhood over the dreams of my childhood, and I understood that there was no other way for us to come together. When I finally held you in my arms, I knew in my heart that I would have waited a hundred years for you. Exactly you. And I would do it all again.

Truth

I first denied, then tried to hide,
but Truth defied and came.
With single-minded confidence she quietly lay claim
to Hint and Doubt—she turned them out—
now nothing is the same.

Sally Bacchetta

Chapter 2

We Really Are Your Parents

Some mothers know, with the first subtle sign, that they carry life within them. They realize something profound has begun, and they can recall the exact moment when they knew they had become part of an organically perfect union. These mothers witness every change their body makes to accommodate the precious new life. They lovingly pat and stroke and whisper love songs to their unborn child. They offer their bodies and minds to sustain the life within, and the great pain they bear is all but forgotten when they first hold their child in their arms and fall in love forever.

Others of us have to trust, often in the absence of any sign whatsoever, that another mother is carrying our child's life within her. We trust that without our knowledge, something profound has begun, and that at the exact right moment, we will become part of a perfectly destined union. We arrange our homes in anticipation of a precious new life, and we lovingly daydream and pray and whisper names for our unborn child. Having offered our bodies to a capricious science, we offer our hearts and hands to the women who carry our children, and the great pain we bear is all but forgotten when we first hold our child in our arms and fall in love forever. All mothers love their children, no matter how they are joined or when they separate.

Your birth mother will always be your birth mother. She will always be the woman who loved you first. She allowed you life, and she will always be the earliest part of who you are. She may be known as birth mother, first mother, natural mother, original mother, and biological mother, but she is not your "real" mother. Your birth mother is not your mother because (I want to say this gently) she chose not to be. She chose to set the course of your life apart from hers. She chose a different role. She chose to love you from a different perspective. She chose to carry you in her heart, not her arms. She chose with love, she chose with courage, she chose with faith. She chose as well as she could, and she made the right choice.

I will always be your mother. I will always be the woman who nurtured you and guided you and helped you develop your life, and I will always be part of who you are. I may be called adoptive mother, second mother, chosen mother, forever mother, but to me, I am simply your mother. I am your mother because I chose to be. I chose to embrace the course of your life, a life entwined with mine. I chose this role. I pursued it. I worked for it. I chose to love you up close. I chose to carry your birth mother in my heart and you in my arms. I chose with love, I chose with courage, I chose with faith. I chose as well as I could, and I made the right choice.

Some fathers talk to their unborn child; other fathers pray that someone else is talking. Some fathers choose names and nicknames and schedule time off; other fathers choose caseworkers and attorneys and schedule home studies. Some fathers cross days off the calendar with growing anticipation, knowing that each pen stroke brings them closer to the day they will help bring their child into the world. Other fathers cross days off the calendar with growing impatience, having no idea which day will be the day that someone else brings their child into the world. Some fathers fall in love forever when they first lay eyes on their child. Other fathers do too. All fathers love their children, no matter how they are joined or when they separate.

Your birth father will always be your birth father. He will always be the man who helped create you, and blood of his blood courses through your veins. He may be called birth father, first father, natural father, original father, and biological father, but he is not your "real" father. He *chose* not to be your father. Whether or not he fully participated in the adoption plan, whether or not he supported your birth mother throughout her pregnancy, whether or not he knew you had been conceived, by his actions he chose not to be your father. By creating a child in whatever circumstance he was in that made adoption the best choice, he chose not to be your father. Whether he chose by decision or by default, he chose to be part of your past. He chose as well as he could, and he made the right choice.

Your father will always be your father. He will always be the man who protected you and guided you and encouraged you to develop your life, and he will always be part of who you are. He is your father. He is your father because he chose to be. Yes, he *chose* to be your father. He fully participated in the adoption plan. He supported me throughout our journey to you, and even before he knew you had been conceived, by his actions he chose to be your father. He chose by decision to be part of your present and future. He chose a life with you. He wanted it, he planned for it, and he worked for it. He chose as well as he could, and he made the right choice.

Your birth parents are real people, and you were really born to them, which makes them both real and parents, but they are not your "real parents." You don't actually have "real" parents and "unreal" parents. You have parents. We are your parents. We use the term "birth parents" to honor them because they gave you life. *Life.* They gave you a life with *us.*

Whether they parented you for years, months, or just a few hours, your birth parents created you and cared for you as well as they could. They loved you and gave you what they were able to give. The most profound expression of their love was acknowledging that they couldn't provide the life they wanted you to have. They knew they couldn't offer you the fullness of opportunity they wanted for you, so as painful as it must have been, they admitted to themselves (and others) that they weren't your forever parents. They knew it.

They knew it as surely as we knew, as soon as we saw you, that you were our forever child. We knew immediately that you were our dream come true, that you were the child we had waited for, that you were *the One*. Right away we knew you as our child. Right away we knew ourselves as your parents. We will always honor your birth parents for giving you life. We will always hold your birth family in our hearts—and we hope you do the same—but we are your parents. *We* are your parents. We *are* your parents. We are *your* parents. We are your *parents*. God brought us together to be a family, and there is no other way it should be.

It wasn't until I became a mother that I realized parenting has very little to do with who created you. When you were born, you took the things I thought were important—bloodlines, family history, physical features—and melted them to nothing in your teeny, tiny, perfect fist. Your teeny, tiny, perfect fist that didn't come from me. It came from them. To me. Their bloodlines, their family history, their physical features—my child.

I know now that parenting has nothing to do with DNA and everything to do with everything else. I know now that parenting is not whose egg let in whose sperm. I know now that parenting is the art of loving someone when they are most unlovable and actually loving them more for trusting you with their worst self. Parenting means leading even when you don't know the way and speaking with authority when you're filled with doubt. It means standing strong when your knees are weak and refusing to compromise what you know is right. It's being ignored in public and adored in private and being OK with both. It's being the first to apologize and the last to eat. It's being so tired you fall asleep standing in the closet. Parenting is beginning each day with the feeling that you're the luckiest person in the world and ending each day with the hope you've made your kids feel the same way.

Being a parent means prying a two-year-old's mouth open and trying to brush her teeth without getting bitten. It's being peed on and spilled on and spit up on and climbed on. Being a parent means having the bathroom door flung open "so my friends can see you pee-pee like a Big Girl." It's having your blouse get unbuttoned in the grocery checkout line and having your skirt lifted up on the way to Communion. Being a parent means looking at a face so streaked with dirt, squash, snot, glue, jelly, or chalk that anyone in her right mind would turn away, and finding it so incredibly beautiful you can't help but kiss it.

We are your parents forever. No matter what you say, no matter what you do, no matter what you discover, reveal, or hide, we remain your parents. Your path is our path. We chose to walk with you through all of your seasons and to love all of who you are. We love who you were when we first held you. We love who you are at this very moment, and we will love you in all the moments yet to be. We love you for your potential. We love you whether or not you love us, whether or not you like us, whether or not you want us to. We love you when you're not looking, when you think no one else does, and even when you don't love yourself, because we are your parents.

We will encourage you, fascinate you, understand you, inspire you, defend you, strengthen you, affirm you, expand you, and otherwise celebrate your person more than anyone else in your life. We will also embarrass you. We will frustrate you. We will make you question yourself. Almost certainly, we will underestimate you, infuriate you, doubt you, challenge you, contradict you, limit you, and otherwise intrude upon your person more than anyone else in your life. And you will do the same to us, because we are your parents and you are our child.

Your birth parents, or thoughts of them, will always be present in your life, sometimes more and sometimes less, sometimes in sync with what you want and sometimes not. Your birth parents, or thoughts of them, will intrigue you, enlighten you, refresh you, center you, and resonate with you differently than anyone else in your life. They will also elude you. They will confound you. They will make you question yourself. Almost certainly, they will anger you, challenge you, frustrate you, and otherwise unsettle your person differently than anyone else in your life. And you, or thoughts of you, will do the same to them. They will always be your birth parents, and you will always be the child born to them. But we are your parents, and you are our child.

Sometimes—particularly during adolescence, when you feel put-upon more often than not—you may be torn between a desire to push us away and a fear that you actually *will* push us away. You may want us to leave you completely alone one minute and wrap you in our arms the next. At breakfast you may wonder if we know anything about anything that matters, and by dinner you may know for certain that we don't. You may lash out with powerful feelings without being sure of their origin. The time may come (it may have already) when you try to hurt us by shouting, "I wish I could find my real parents!" or "I bet my real parents would let me …" do whatever it is we won't let you do. And because *we are* your parents, we will let you say it. We will not try to silence you. We will not deny the intensity of your feelings. We will respect your struggle. We will do our best to understand and to trust when you need some space. And when you need to, we will let you push us out. Not too far and not for too long, but out enough for you to breathe, reflect, and come to terms with what's on your mind. And then, when the time is right, we will gently gather you in again. We will gather you in and bring you back. We will always bring you back, because we are your parents.

We want to sit with you and listen as you describe the complexities of life … of adoption … of *your* life and *your* adoption experience. We want you to tell us how you feel and what you think. We will do our best to understand the enormous challenges of missing people you never knew, growing up without your siblings, and juggling your identity as our child with your identity as theirs. We want you to ask questions. We want you to push back. Dig deeper. Talk about what you want but don't have. Tell us what you imagine. Tell us how you feel about it. We will honor your feelings and accept them as real and important and potent. We want to love you through your anger, pain, and confusion, and teach you to manage it. We want to affirm you, and sometimes we'll succeed. Sometimes we'll get it right. Sometimes we'll be just who you need, and at other times we won't. Other times we'll fail miserably. Other times we'll seem alien. When that happens, it will be up to you to step up and take responsibility for yourself. It will be up to you to live fully in the present and move beyond the past. We will never abandon you. We will never wish you gone. We will never regret adopting you. We will never stop loving you. We will take you as far as we can because we are your parents. The rest is up to you.

Some people who were adopted harbor a secret fear that it could happen again, either literally or symbolically. Some adoptees are driven to prove again and again that they are worthy of their parents' love or worthy of being "chosen." Perhaps knowing the arduous path their parents took to adoption, they feel pressure to live up to an ideal. My child, you don't have to prove anything. You don't have to "earn" membership in the family. We held a place for you—exactly you—in our hearts and our home even before you were born. We love you as only parents can love. Completely. We love you for everything you are and everything you make of us. We love you for what you bring to the family. You are a miracle to us. We love your mind and your spirit. We love your questions. We love what you say. We love the unsaid things we read on your face. We love looking at you, holding you, hearing you. We love you, and we know that we belong together now and forever—good, bad, happy, sad—because we are your parents and you are our child.

To us, being adopted is no more or less important than any other thing about you. Adoption has had a greater impact on your life than some other things, but it has no bearing on the way we love you. We don't love you either less or more because you were adopted. We love you with fullness because of who you are, not because of how you were born. You are not our "adopted child"; you're our child. We don't expect more from you because you were adopted, but neither are we going to expect less. We love you too much to ever let you use adoption as an excuse.

We will almost surely disagree with some of the choices you make, and we will almost surely be upset by some of your decisions. As your parents, we have an obligation to you, to ourselves, and to your birth parents to point that out and encourage you to make better choices. But we love you unconditionally. You don't have to worry that we will ever regret adopting you, no matter how turbulent your toddler or teenage years may be! We understand that your feelings toward us and adoption and your birth family may change over time. We understand that some things may be difficult to express. We understand that you may not think about adoption much at all. We also understand the myriad anxieties, insecurities, sentimentalities, wounds, betrayals, and elations of humanity that have nothing at all to do with adoption. We fully expect to be bowled over (perhaps more than once) by some confession or revelation of yours. Trust me, we can take it. Being a family means that our bond is strong enough to hold us together no matter what happens. We are your parents—forever—and we're not going anywhere.

Even smart people say dumb things, especially when they're not familiar with a topic or situation. Unfortunately, some people misunderstand the bond between adoptive parents and their children. Some are genuinely interested in the topic of adoption and they word their questions clumsily (even rudely) without meaning to offend. Other people seem to think nothing of mining your privacy to satisfy their curiosity, as if you're an exhibit or a sideshow. If you haven't already, at some point in the future you will no doubt overhear insensitive comments and questions. Some of them may even be directed to you. I hope you realize that these comments reveal much about the people who make them and nothing at all about you or our family. You decide how you want to respond, if at all. You aren't responsible for educating the populace about your birth story or adoption in general. You have no more obligation than anyone else to discuss your personal business with strangers or even acquaintances. You have our full support either way.

Here are some of the questions and comments I've fielded as an adoptive parent. Some are amusing, some are shocking, and some just left me speechless.

> ***"It's too bad you couldn't have children of your own."***
>
> What I said: "This *is* my child, as much as your child is yours. This is my child emotionally, legally, unconditionally, and forever. Adoption is the way we came together, but the life we live together every day is what makes us family."
>
> ***"I just don't understand how a mother could give her baby away."***
>
> What I said: "I think I know what you mean, but if you say it like that, it's clear that you don't understand. Birth mothers don't give their babies away. The decision to relinquish is extremely personal, regardless of the circumstances of the pregnancy and birth. Some birth mothers are blessed with family support. Others are isolated, maybe abused or threatened, and may hide their

pregnancy. Their adoption plan may consist only of a brief phone call to an agency after the baby has been born. Some mothers are under tremendous sociopolitical pressure to leave their child at an orphanage. It often feels less like making a choice and more like fulfilling an expectation. I don't think it's possible to truly understand a mother's path to making an adoption plan for her child."

"How much did she cost?

What I said: "Nothing. Love is free."

"Are you afraid his real parents will try to find him?

What I said: "No … we haven't lost him. We are his 'real parents.' His birth parents made the decision to relinquish their parental rights in order to give him a quality of life they weren't able to provide. Although they will always love him, they have no more legal claim to parent him than you do."

"She is so lucky to have you."

What I said: "No, we're the lucky ones!"

"Are you going to tell her that she's adopted?"

What I said: "She *was* adopted, and she knows it. We talk about her birth parents and her adoption in a way that is meaningful for her. She knows that adoption is the way our family came together."

"I would never have known that he was adopted."

What I said: "Oh … ? How would you know?"

"It takes a special person to adopt a child."

What I said: "Not a child as special as this. Her birth mother is special. It takes a *really* special person to carry a child in their body for nine months and then entrust them to someone else. I appreciate the compliment, but I'm no more special than any parent."

"I would have considered adopting if I couldn't have children of my own."

What I said: "Well, adoption isn't right for everyone. It's been an incredible experience for our family. We're very glad we adopted, and we can't imagine our life without our kids."

Being a parent means giving more than you think you can more often than you thought you would and still wanting, more than anything, to have more to give. We are your parents—your "real" parents—because there is nothing we want more.

Into My Own

One of my wishes is that those dark trees,
So old and firm they scarcely show the breeze,
Were not, as 'twere, the merest mask of gloom,
But stretched away unto the edge of doom.

I should not be withheld but that someday
Into their vastness I should steal away,
Fearless of ever finding open land,
Or highway where the slow wheel pours the sand.

I do not see why I should e'er turn back,
Or those should not set forth upon my track
To overtake me, who should miss me here
And long to know if still I held them dear.

They would not find me changed from him they knew—
Only more sure of all I thought was true.

Robert Frost

Chapter 3

I Regret What I Can't Give You

I can't replace anything you lost when the first voice you ever heard stopped talking to you, when the heartbeat you pulsed with for nine months suddenly went away, when in one moment, the only world you knew vanished. I can't give you her. I knew when I first held you that you cried for her. You cried for her, but she didn't come. You reached for her and the native scents and sounds and touch that you knew, and you found me instead, with my different arms, my different sway, my different world. I felt you indignant at finding nothing of her in my touch or my voice or my home, and no matter how you cried for her, she didn't come.

But I did. Again and again I came to you. Again and again I soothed you, fed you, cleaned you, cradled you, held you, wanted you, loved you. I loved you because I wanted to. I loved you because I was meant to. I loved you because I had to, because you awakened a love that exists in me only for you. I loved you immediately and completely and without expectation, and when you were ready, you loved me back. When you were ready, you accepted what I had to give you. When you were ready, you reached for me because you wanted *me*.

Our adoption attorney (himself an adoptive parent) once said to me, "Information is limited even in the best of circumstances. That's the reality of adoption." I used to think he was referring to the information available to prospective adoptive parents in the initial stage of "matching." For example, while waiting for you, your father and I periodically got calls from the agency along the lines of "We're working with a birth mother who's due to deliver any day now. 'Mom' is eighteen, Hispanic, and her parents are with her. She has some kind of hereditary blood disorder … we're not sure what. She did not have prenatal care, so we don't know whether or not the baby also has it. We know that the baby is biracial. We don't know anything about the birth father. She's reviewed your profile and is interested in meeting you."

We'd hang up the phone, huddle up for a prayer, and do our best to figure out if this was the Call. My first instinct was always to say yes, but that was selfish. I was so eager to be a mother I convinced myself that every call was divinely inspired, and to say no would be to walk away from the Child We Were Meant To Be With. Obviously, I was wrong. Because when we got the call about you, your father and I both knew it was right. With limited information about your birth parents, their families, and your prenatal care, we knew it was You. Somehow we knew. I guess our attorney was right. Information is limited even in the *best* of circumstances.

I will always regret what I can't give you. That's the reality of being a parent. I regret that I can't give you details about some very personal, possibly important things, like the play-by-play of the day you were born or the whole of your birth parents' journey to adoption. I regret that I can't give you a more peaceful beginning or an easier transition from your first mother to me, and I wonder if your first separation affected you in ways I don't realize.

I can't give you siblings who look like you. Pictures of your ancestors. A genetic match. Does that matter to you? Is your life less complete because of it? I regret that I can't give you certainty about some things I'd like to be certain about. There is so much I don't know about your birth parents and the beginning of your life, and uncertainty about the information I do have. I know so little about your birth father. A name, an age, a physical description—he's half of who you are, and I know more about most grocery cashiers than I do about him. What does he like? What *is* he like? Is he like you? Are you very much like your birth parents, or not much at all? I can't say which of your talents and temperament are nature and which are nurture. I can't lay your baby pictures next to snapshots of your birth parents at the same age and remark how much you look like them. Is any of this important to you? Will it be important at some point?

I have forgotten more of my family history than you will ever know of yours, and my inability to know your history makes mine seem both more and less significant. Names, dates, places, and events that I may otherwise not care about become important to me when I realize we have so few from your past. I can't give you the organic belonging that comes from being raised within your biological family. Some of our physical differences are obvious to the most casual observer, and I regret that a piece of your personal story is broadcast, wholesale, wherever we go. You will meet people who think you belong less because you were adopted, people who place a mental asterisk next to your picture in their mind. Sadly, there are people who will always think of you as my *adopted* child. I don't. I hope you don't either.

In her book *Keys to Parenting an Adopted Child*, Kathy Lancaster, Ph.D., writes, "All children struggle at one time or another with issues related to their adoption." And, "All adopted children deal with such questions as 'Why didn't my first parents want me?' and 'Who am I, really?'" I believe the search for Self is a universal drive, possibly instinctive. From time to time we all ponder our place in the larger world; we all question the meaning of life in general and our lives in particular. But as Lancaster points out, "For adopted people, a major difference in their search for self is that a part of them has been cut away." She writes that people who were adopted experience a "sense of a lost past and lost relationships."

I regret the loss inherent in your life. I regret that you probably won't find everything you search for. In truth, I probably won't find everything I search for either, but it seems that any closed doors in my past can eventually be opened if I want to invest enough time, energy, and resources into picking the lock. But for you, some doors are destined to remain closed forever, no matter what you do. I'm sorry about that. I'm sorry I can't offer you anything more than support and perspective.

Even supposedly-open adoption is strangely murky, and I'm not certain that what I believe to be true about your origins actually is true. Open information is carefully worded, and closed information is closely guarded. Correspondence with the agency and your birth family is worded so carefully it feels so darn deliberate. It's as if your birth mother and I are logrolling, both of us working so hard to keep our balance that we don't look anywhere but at you for fear of losing our footing. In one accidental moment, I learn something about your birth father that I probably shouldn't know, and realizing her mistake, your birth mother wobbles and looks stricken. I pretend not to notice and pretend I didn't hear, but I did notice, and I did hear, and now I'm rolling that log as fast as I can so I don't slip off into the icy water.

It hurts me to know that you struggle with unsolvable riddles. It hurts me to know you have questions about yourself that I can't help you answer. Sometimes I think I want to know more. Sometimes I think I want to soak up as much as I can for you, but I'm also afraid of what I may find out and afraid of what it may cost me or us or your birth family. I'm torn between respect for their privacy and a desire to give you everything I can about your biological roots. I want to know far more than I ask about, holding back out of fear that if I push too hard or want too much, your birth mother might get spooked and cut off all contact. Your birth parents made the adoption plan they made for you with certain expectations of privacy, and they deserve to have that upheld. I won't violate that covenant, not even to help you.

There's a larger issue, too: the issue of faith—my faith in you. Here you are—vibrant and wonderful, fully formed yet still evolving—creating a life without your original history. I watch you becoming who you will without knowing who you were or who you might have become. Your Being suggests that history is ultimately insignificant, for you know little of yours and yet you are very much a force in this world. You change the world by who you are, not who you came from, and you change my living history just by being yourself. You have made every day since we came together the most important day of my life, and I believe in your ability to be whole without all the details of your history. I trust that you will be all right. I regret that I can't make your search for Self easier or more comfortable, but I have faith that you can make it fruitful, however you define it.

Every time you fill out a form that asks for your medical history, you will be reminded that other people know more about their history than you do. You will be confronted with the assumption, the *expectation*, that you know something as vital and intimate as your body's medical lineage. I want you to recognize that the error in this assumption lies with the medical community and its form, not with you. What's "wrong" is the form, not you. I hope you will speak up and suggest the form be changed to make it inclusive of adoptive situations. So many families are formed through adoption; it's past time for the medical community, the education establishment, and government organizations to demonstrate greater sensitivity to the realities of adoption. Certainly, your doctor needs to know why you don't have certain familial medical history, but other than that, it's your prerogative if, when, and with whom you want to share your beginnings. You shouldn't have to declare it, impersonally and by default, with blank spaces on a waiting room form.

I regret that I can't unburden your heart. I'm sure there are things on your mind that I don't know about and places within yourself where I can't go. I'm OK with that. There are such places in me, too. I hope you go there because you want to, not because you think you must. I hope you know I want to hear your questions, whether or not I have answers. I want you to know that I respect your separateness, even when I wish you felt closer. I want you to remember, in case you ever feel so separate from me that you doubt we can bridge the gap between us, I will always meet you halfway. I would gladly reach more than halfway, but I can't live your half for you. I haven't had your experiences, and I can't give you insight I don't have.

You are you, no matter who your parents are. If your birth parents had raised you, the details of your life would be different, but you would still be you. Maybe you would feel closer to them than you do to me, maybe you would feel less connected to them than you do to me. You might be more or less open with them, feel more or less like them, understand each other either more or less than you and I do. But you would be you and they would be they, and you would each be separate from the other.

You may assume I know how you feel or what's going on in your mind, but I don't, and your birth parents wouldn't either. That's right. The challenge of understanding isn't unique to the adoptive relationship; it's a universal parent-child thing, even a human being to human being thing. I'm sorry for the times I misunderstand or misinterpret your feelings, and I'm sorry for the times I project my own onto you. I regret the times I lack sufficient clarity or sensitivity to help you heal your mind and heart. I will always regret what I can't give you. That's the reality of being a parent. There are things I simply can't do or make happen, no matter how much I'd like to. And there are things I will choose not to do, no matter how much you want me to do them. I realize this may cause tremendous stress between us or around us, and I'm sorry for that. I hope you know I always have your best interest in mind. I hope you know that I love you completely. Imperfectly, maybe, but with my whole heart.

My child, I rejoice that there is so much I *can* give you. Unconditional love. Time and attention. A permanent place in our family. I can give you absolute certainty about some very important, very personal things, like a play-by-play of the day we brought you home or our journey to adoption. I can point out how very much alike we are in talent and temperament, and how very much we differ. I can give you interest and enthusiasm. I can teach you the joy of discovery and the beauty of accomplishment. I can give you guidance, laughter, and affirmation. I can give you respect. I can give you a safe place, a secure home, forever love.

I rejoice that I can give you expectations and the belief that you can meet them. I can give you responsibility with the opportunity to fulfill it. It's an honor to watch you develop confidence through your achievements, whether finally picking up your caterpillar rattle or finally picking out which college to attend. It's a joy to see you develop compassion and determination and creativity, and to know that I am co-author of your developing self. I'm grateful for the chance to share my values and perspective with you, to help shape your impressions of God and life and love, and to participate in your personal evolution.

I am grateful for whatever information I can give you about your birth family and your earliest days, and I will share as much as I can about your personal past. It's yours to know, my child. It's yours. At the same time, I appreciate the unique freedom of not knowing. As one adoptive mother I know put it, "The lack of family history means that we are free from undue expectations and each of my children is free to unfold as an individual."

Some of our physical differences are obvious even to strangers, but so are some of our similarities. People see in the way we treat each other the overwhelming love, loyalty, respect, and gratitude we count among the blessings of adoption. There are customs and mannerisms, expressions of speech, stories and jokes that are unique to our family. It's a thrill for me to see and hear them from you. I'm also delighted by the pieces of your past that you've carried forward, perhaps unknowingly.

I rejoice that some pages of your personal story are not broadcast, wholesale, wherever we go. Certain things about your adoption live only in my experience, and I will cherish them as long as I live. I rejoice that I can give you the unseverable bond of belonging that comes with membership in our family. You are my child, and I will always love you as fully and protect you as fiercely as any mother ever did her child. I rejoice that I can give you myself, for we belong together. I feel it every time I look at you; I hope you feel it, too.

I love knowing that I can give you the life your birth parents wanted you to have. I can give you the care and balance and emotional support and consistency they wanted for you but were unable to give. When I first held you, I was acutely aware of having been "chosen" and was surprised by the profound obligation I felt to your birth mother. Not in the sense of a quid pro quo—she was an absolute gem and hadn't done anything to make me feel this way—but in the sense that she entrusted her personal miracle to ME. It seemed vitally important that I honor her sacrifice by raising you well. It was visceral ... and quite unexpected. I rejoice that I can give that to you and to them.

I will always be grateful for the sacred trust that is the core of our relationship. Your birth mother trusted me with you, and that has always been extremely important to me. I'm glad I can give that knowledge to you. Whatever else you know or don't know about your biological parents, you know they made an adoption plan with faith in me and you.

Chapter 4

You Are Not Different Because You Were Adopted (You Are Different Because You Are You)

Before we can talk about whether or not you're different because you are adopted, we have to dispense with the notion that you are adopted, because in fact, you're not. That's right. You are not adopted. You *were* adopted. Adoption only happens once. It's not a recurring event or an ongoing condition. It's an action that was taken sometime in the past. You were adopted—past tense. You are my child. You are reading these words. You think and feel and decide and express yourself every day; these are ongoing and repeatable, because you are living your life—present tense. You *were* adopted. *Past tense.*

It's likely that your feelings about adoption will emerge and reemerge throughout your life, and you may at times grieve certain aspects of adoption and celebrate others, but the initial separation and subsequent joining that is adoption only happened once. It may have been incredibly significant (or not), but it isn't who you are. It isn't who you may become. You are not adopted. You *were* adopted.

Why is that distinction important? Because in order to fully develop and love your Self, you need to understand that you are more than the sum of your life's events. You need to know that your potential extends far beyond anything that has happened or will happen to you, with you, for you, by you. As long as you think of yourself as being different because you were adopted, you will *feel* different, and you will presume that it's because you were adopted. And since adoption isn't the norm, and since the adoption decision was out of your control, it's an easy and dangerous jump from "I was adopted" to "I'm different and abnormal. I have no control over the problems in my life, because I was adopted, and therefore destined to be dysfunctional."

Well, guess what? The only thing you can truly attribute to being adopted is the fact that you have different genetic material in your cells than your parents do. That's it. Everything else about you is subject to the same environmental forces that shape us all. You have the same opportunities as the rest of us to grow, mature, and adapt. We all deal with stress, insecurity, uncertainty, anger, loss, grief, fantasies of the perfect life—what's different for you is that you have adoption to pin it on. If you hadn't been adopted, you would feel those things about something else, probably your friendships, schoolwork, job situations, falling in love, breaking up, buying a house, or the death of a loved one, like the rest of us. If you hadn't been adopted, you would still feel those feelings; they would simply be born of different experiences.

"The child is father of the man."[1] Every one of us is a product of our earlier Self. Who you are today began with who you were yesterday, and who you were yesterday began with who you were the day before yesterday, and so on for all of your days before that. Who you are today comprises who you were on every day before now. No one thing makes or breaks who you are. Adoption is one part of who you are. Just like your name is one part of who you are, every experience you've ever had is part of who you are. The fact that you were adopted is a detail of your life, and facts themselves are neutral. You assign meaning to the facts of your life. You determine the weight and significance of your experiences, and you decide what to carry forward with you.

Being adopted doesn't make you anything other than my child. Your relationships with me and your father, your siblings, and peers are far more influential in contouring your personality than the fact that you were adopted. The opportunities you have for meaningful achievement in school, athletics, music, religion, and your community contribute more to who you are than does your primal separation. People learn more about you by the way you handle challenge and success than by learning that you were adopted.

Adoption happened in your past, and you have lived the bulk of your life since then. If adoption is a big clumsy obstacle in your way now, it is you who have hauled it forward. It is you who has blocked your own path, and you are the only one who can clear it. Ultimately, it is what you do, not what has been done to you, that determines Who You Are. You are not adopted.

You may have heard or read about the ways some people think adoption makes you different. Let's talk about some of them, starting with this personal profile. This is just for you, so spend some time reflecting on each question and then answer as honestly as you can.

Do you become anxious or depressed about social situations when you are unsure of the Rules?

Do you avoid intimacy and personal commitment because you're afraid of being rejected or abandoned?

Have you struggled with your identity?

Do you wonder if you're a good/bad kid because you want to be or because you think you have to be?

Do you feel like you have to continually prove that you're worth keeping?

Do you befriend misfits? Is it because you're compassionate or because you see yourself as one?

Do you blur the lines between daring and self-destructive? Between loyal and codependent?

Do you wonder who you really are?

Do you wonder if you will ever feel truly complete?

Do you experience separation anxiety or fears of abandonment?

Are you troubled by periods of self-doubt or low self-esteem?

Have you ever fantasized that one day your "real" parents will find you and declare their love, pledge their undying devotion, and whisk you away to live happily ever after in their jeweled palace / tropical paradise / chocolate factory / space station / underwater city?

If you answered "yes" to three or more of those questions, you were most certainly adopted. Or most certainly not. You see, people are more alike than different. Whether born and raised within our biological family, begun as a donated egg or conceived through in vitro fertilization, carried by a surrogate, remanded to foster care, placed in an orphanage, or adopted at birth, we are more alike than different. Our doubts and fears are more alike than different. Our hopes and dreams are more alike than different. At some point, many children raised by their biological parents actually entertain the fantasy that they are adopted and one day their "real" parents will find them! You are not different because you were adopted.

Don't believe the "adoption as handicap" propaganda. Some people will tell you that adoption somehow diminishes your ability to fully experience all that life has to offer. That's nonsense. The only thing that diminishes your ability to fully experience all that life has to offer is your decision to limit yourself. The fact that you were adopted doesn't make you either more or less functional than anyone else. It doesn't predispose you to develop alcoholism or severe depression, and you aren't more likely to suffer from poor self-esteem than someone who wasn't adopted.[2] Adoption doesn't make you more likely to smoke, get pregnant while in high school, sell drugs, steal cars, or place your own child for adoption. Neither does it make you more heroic, more popular, more ambitious, hardworking, intriguing, or talented than anyone else. Your triumphs and failures don't come more easily or less, or mean any more or any less because you were adopted. You are no more different because you were adopted than you are different for having a family that loves you. Some people have that; many don't.

Have you heard that most adoptees feel restless, that they feel incomplete, unfinished, not quite whole? That's true for some. However, many people who were adopted don't feel that way at all, and plenty of people who were *not* adopted *do* feel that way. Many people—adopted and not—spend huge amounts of time searching for their roots. And other people—adopted and not—couldn't care less about theirs. Many people—adopted and not—are very closely knit with their parents and siblings. Other people—adopted and not—rarely speak with theirs. Day after day people—adopted and not—wander the world in search of meaning. Day after day people—adopted and not—find religion, renounce religion, question their faith, confirm their faith, triumph, fail, persevere, give up, feel lost, are found, stand together, stand alone, fall, rise again, seek understanding, achieve inner peace. Programs for juvenile delinquency, drug and alcohol abuse, depression, anxiety, and eating disorders are clogged with people who were adopted. *And with those who weren't.* You are not different because you were adopted.

Although you share some very real and possibly important feelings and challenges with other people who were adopted, the word "adopted" doesn't describe you. It's not your name. It doesn't belong as a prefix on everything you do. You're not the adopted valedictorian of your high school or the adopted principal violinist in the orchestra, the adopted algebra teacher or the adopted landscaper. You're not an adopted pharmacist or an adopted priest. "Adopted" isn't a qualifier like "award-winning" or "certified," and having been adopted neither augments nor diminishes your abilities or achievements.

There is no shortage of expert opinion promoting the "adoptee as victim" perspective, no shortage of people claiming that the primal separation dooms adopted children, without exception, to a lifetime of emotional mayhem. You don't have to look far to find this thinking propagated in books, magazines, support groups, Web sites, and online forums. Sadly, some people do experience intense, long-term emotional pain related to their adoption experience. I know adult adoptees and birth parents who do feel victimized by adoption. I know some who feel guilty and manipulated and regretful. I know some adoptees who struggle with fears of abandonment, separation, rejection, criticism, uncertainty, and loss.

And I know plenty who don't.

Although some people experience adoption as a monumental loss, others don't. Some people never move beyond the pain of adoption, while others do. Even though some people believe that they struggle and suffer and feel different because they were adopted, many people who were not adopted struggle just as much and suffer just as much and feel just as different.

Many adoptees regard adoption as the gift of a lifetime. An adult adoptee once told me, "If I ever meet my birth parents, I'm going to kiss their feet and thank them for having the sense to place me for adoption. They were just teenagers! I don't think they could have done it, and in the end, I probably would have gone into foster care and been shuffled around a million times. Instead I was raised in a stable, loving family by parents who had the maturity and wisdom to parent properly. I love my parents, and I'm forever grateful to my birth parents!"

I know adult adoptees who don't feel any unusual fears or emotional imbalance and rarely think about the fact that they were adopted, having always felt a deep sense of belonging with their parents and siblings. One adoptee friend says she has a fairly casual curiosity about her birth parents but no longing to meet them or delve into her genetic medical history. She says, "I've never felt like damaged goods or any of the things I sometimes hear other adoptees talk about. I have a great life and I love my family. I'm curious about my birth family in the same way a lot of people are curious about great-grandparents or great-great-grandparents. I think of them as part of my bloodline more than a distinct part of me or my life."

I know birth parents who credit adoption for saving them and their cherished child from a terrible circumstance and birth parents (like yours) who consider adoption a blessing. One birth mother I know says that for her, adoption was redemption. She became pregnant while "rocketing down the path to self-destruction". She knew she wasn't ready to be a mother, and she saw adoption as an opportunity to do something positive and meaningful. "I felt good about adopting my baby out because I knew I was helping him and helping someone who couldn't have kids. I've seen him a few times, and it makes me sad that he doesn't know who I really am, but I know he's happy and he has a good life. That means a lot to me."

Are adoptees victims? It depends who you ask. Is adoption a perverse disassembling of people and relationships? It depends who you ask. Only you can decide what adoption means for you. Your truth is yours. You don't have to share it, explain it, or defend it to anyone. I want you to remember that an individual truth isn't a universal truth just because people repeat it. No matter how many people say it, no matter how many times, no matter how many ways, it remains an individual truth. Everyone has their own take on reality.

My question to the "adoption is evil" people is this: If it's true that adoption sentences adoptees to an unwinnable marathon for identity and integration, for attachment and belonging, how can it be that most adopted teens are as deeply attached to their parents as non-adopted teens? Why do most of them say they feel positively about their identity? How can it be that for most adopted adolescents, adoption is something they accept as a fact of life?[3] And why are so many people who were *not* adopted exhausting themselves in the same race for meaning? Why do so many people who were *not* adopted experience a similar search for meaning and feelings of alienation and depression similar to what some adoptees report?

The answer is that adoption doesn't make you different. You were not born into a preordained set of feelings or expectations, and adoption doesn't supplant free will or personal responsibility. Adoption doesn't automatically set you up for a lifetime of unresolved loss and identity confusion. You came into the world with mental and emotional tools; it's up to you to learn how to use them. Adoption itself doesn't make you different from people who weren't adopted, and it doesn't make you the same as other people who were.

If you let it, adoption can become an easy catch-all for anything you don't like about yourself or your life. Think about it: If you make adoption responsible for everything that's wrong in your life, then you're not responsible. If you can trace all of your problems to being adopted, you don't have to trace them to your own decisions and behaviors. If adoption "did this" to you (whatever "this" is), you are free from any expectation to change and make "this" better. If you think of adoption as something that injured your emotional Self and made you forever different in some significant way, you will feel injured and forever different, and you will interact with the world that way.

I know an adoptee who learned as a teen that he had two younger biological siblings, both of whom were being raised by his birth mother. He never had any contact with his birth family, and he grew up blaming "adoption-related unresolved feelings of rejection and resentment" for his three failed marriages and his ongoing difficulty keeping a job and meeting financial obligations. He decided early on that adoption was powerful and he himself was powerless, and he lived his life in a way that made it seem so. He fulfilled his own prophecy.

Adoption is but one point in your personal constellation. If you had been raised in your biological family, that too would have been but one point. If you had been raised in a different country or a different culture, that would have been but one point. Your laugh, your frown, the way you think about the world, the look in your eyes when you're excited or happy or sad, the size of your imagination, your first thought in the morning, the goals you set for yourself—these things make you different; adoption doesn't.

If you had been raised in your biological family, you would still be different. You might find deep similarities with people who are culturally and biologically "your people," but within your biological family, you would be individual and different. Everyone is different. Even siblings don't grow up in the same family. Your place in the birth order, your gender, the sound of your name, the color of your bedroom walls, your favorite book, all of these things make you different, but they also make you who you are. You are not different because you were adopted. You are different because you are you.

You are not different because you were adopted, but your life is. As you journey from beginning to end, you will discover obstacles and pitfalls that are unique to the adoptive experience. You will be confronted with ignorance, stereotypes, and bias about adoption, and each time you will have to choose between correcting and educating or letting the ignorance stand unchallenged. You will label and be labeled, and you will have to decide for yourself which words divide and which unite—birth mother, natural mother, first mother, real mother, raised, sin, bastard, given up, given away, illegitimate, love child, relinquished, placed, forever, abandoned, secret, rescued, unwanted, chosen—you will have to decide which words have meaning for you. Does the word "adopted" impact your life more than the word "Italian" or "Jew" or "female"? Does it matter more or less to you than being loved and raised by parents who would lay down their lives for you? What about the term "given up"? Is that what you think your adoption was about? Were you "given up"? Are you "illegitimate"? Are you "a shame"? Are you intelligent, compassionate, skilled, motivated, dedicated? You decide which words matter to you.

When people say hurtful things about adoption and you and your birth parents (trust me, someone will), what are you going to say? I guarantee that at some point someone will openly criticize your birth mother and will pass judgment on the difficult decisions she made. What are you going to say? Are you going to say anything at all? That's up to you. You're living this life; you have to decide which battles to fight. You're not obligated to defend your birth mother or me or anyone else. I want you to feel obligated to yourself. I want you to be smart enough to realize that there are hurtful things to be said about every one of us, adopted or not. I want you to be secure enough in your Self to realize that mean-spirited comments reveal more about the people who make them than they do about you.

You will meet people who think you should be grateful that your father and I "took you in" and people who will expect you to spend your life proving your worth. Virtual strangers will ask intrusive questions and expect you to share intimate details about your life, even as most of them would never dream of speaking as candidly about their own. Some people will lower their voices to a whisper when they say the word "adopted" or look at you sympathetically if the topic comes up, as if they're talking about something embarrassing or shameful. You are not different because you were adopted, even though some people will treat you as if you are.

Because you were adopted, your family is different from many of the families you read about or see on television or in the movies. Adoptive families are sorely underrepresented in the mainstream media, so your life looks different from most of what you see. However, if you spend much time with other adoptive families or adoption-focused clubs, blogs, social networks, or forums, you'll realize that in those arenas, biological families seem different.

Your life is different because there are people from your past who may surface, unbidden, at any point. You may unexpectedly receive an e-mail from a woman claiming to be your birth mother. You may meet someone at college who turns out to be a biological sibling. You may answer the phone the morning of your wedding and find yourself talking to your birth father who only recently found out about you. I can't prepare you for all of the potential challenges of a life that is different because you were adopted, but I hope you will talk to me when your life is too different. I promise I will always do my best to help you feel whole. I promise I will listen and do my best to understand. I promise I will share with you what I can. I promise I won't think any differently about you than I do now.

My child, because you were adopted, you will be gifted in ways you can't imagine. You will experience joy that takes your breath away. You will be touched by kindness and generosity you wouldn't have known otherwise. People will share themselves with you in profound and unexpected ways, and you will be astonished by the human capacity for grace. You will find friendship in places you never would have looked, and it will change you forever. You may one day look at your child as I look at you and be moved beyond words by the understanding of how very much your birth mother must have loved you to be able to let you go. Yes, your life is profoundly different because you were adopted.

Chapter 5

To My Daughter / To My Son

Sometimes when I look at you, I cry. I cry in thanksgiving. I cry with relief. I weep with a joy I can't contain, overcome by the reality of you. A mother friend once said to me, "When you have kids, you fall in love with them all over again every day." I know she's right. I fall in love with you every time I look in your eyes, your unflinching eyes that see me more clearly than I see myself and love me anyway. I fall in love with you every time I hear your voice, your voice that finds me easily even in a crowd. I fall in love with you every time I hug you, wipe your face, stroke your hair, hold your hand. I fall in love with you all over again all the time.

I've told you that adoption doesn't make you different but it does make your life different in certain ways (see chapter 4). Do you know it does that for me, too? My experience of motherhood is different than it would be if you were my biological child. There are differences born of struggle and differences born of bounty. I fought hard for the privilege of motherhood, and I love you with a covenant forged during a long and painful struggle. I love you with gratitude for the women who loved you first. I

44

love you with humility rooted in your birth mother's sacrifice. I love you with awe, aware of how close I came to not being your mother. I love you with wisdom ripened during the slow years I waited for you. I love you triumphantly, because I am your mother, and you are my child, and "we" are a miracle. Yes, I love you differently because you were adopted.

Our bond is different than it would be if you came from my body. It's no less permanent or less binding, it's just different. Being an adoptive parent means I have to get up close and personal with the notion that you are not "mine." I don't look for myself in your face. I don't listen for myself in your voice. I don't look for signs that you've inherited your father's athleticism or my aptitude for music. I don't presume to understand you as I might if you were my biological child. You carry memories I may never know of or understand. You sometimes act in ways I don't recognize. You are a bit of a mystery to me.

The truth is that all children are somewhat mysterious to adults. All children surprise and startle their parents from time to time, and it's not uncommon to hear moms and dads wonder aloud, "Where did *that* come from?" The difference for me is that I wonder: "*Who* did that come from? Why now? What does it mean?"

I have to admit that in the quietest corner of my brain lurks the fear that adoption may have affected you in ways neither of us realizes. Sometimes I have to consciously tease out adoption from my knee-jerk thinking when you challenge me in ways that are typical (aren't they?) and healthy (I hope). When you sass me, when you're stubborn, when you "freak out" if I go somewhere without you, there's a part of me that wonders if it has anything to do with the fact that you were adopted. Even as I reassure your father that your behavior is perfectly normal for your age or a natural response to parental interference, I'm secretly groping for my own assurance.

All parents have questions. All parents second-guess themselves. All parents doubt. Adoption morphs normal parental doubt into something stronger and more pervasive. It's like parental doubt on steroids. Adoption adds a layer, a nuance, an extra variable to every facet of parenting. If I find you sneaking out of the house at night when you're thirteen, I might react differently because you were adopted than I would if you were my biological child. I might read into it; I might be more concerned. Without wanting to, I might worry that you inherited some predisposition toward defiance or self-abuse or antisocial behavior from one or both of your birth parents. I might wonder what prenatal or adoption-related influences are at play. It might not make sense to you, and it's definitely not fair, but that's really how it is.

I *know* what *I* did as a child; I know the risks I took and the dumb things I did that I somehow lived to tell about. I know which decisions were my worst, and I know exactly where they took me. I don't know any of that about your birth parents. I don't know the inborn vulnerabilities and tendencies of your genetic family. I don't know if you're genetically wired to take risks or take drugs or hear voices, and the not knowing gnaws at me. It's my fear of the unknown. I can't protect you unless I know what I'm up against. If you've ever thought I overreacted to something you did, now you know why.

I know many parents who are challenged by a biological child's disrespect, general defiance, lying, eating disorder, depression, poor performance in school, self-abuse, underage drinking, promiscuity, or other dangerous behavior. Adoption doesn't make you any more or less likely to self-destruct. But when biological parents think immaturity, peer pressure, curiosity, experimentation, or stress, I have to also consider unresolved adoption grief, latent hostility, self-loathing, identity crisis, and reactive attachment disorder. Med students are taught the phrase "When you hear hoofbeats, think horses, not zebras" as a reminder to rule out common causes before jumping to the rare and exotic. As an adoptive parent, sometimes all I see are the zebras.

I know adoptive parents who struggle to raise a child whose personality and temperament are different from their own. Frankly, I'm delighted by our differences. I think it frees both of us to evolve naturally, individually and together, without expectation or assumption. I'm proud of you and the ways you surprise me. You show me ways of thinking about things and looking at the world that are different from what I know, and it keeps me grounded in the moment. It keeps me from falling into rigid patterns of expectation. I think it makes me a better mother.

Your birth parents will always be important in your life regardless of the relationship you have with me or the relationship you have with them, if you have one at all. I believe their absence impacts you as powerfully as their presence, and the fact that they are not here is as important as the reason. No matter how integrated and attached you and I are, growing up without your birth parents is a tremendous loss of potential. Without a biological connection, you lose the potential for answers, relationships (with your birth parents and your extended biological family), and affirmation of who you are or once were. You lose the potential for multigenerational influences, genetic medical history, and organic attachment. You may not feel that loss right now, but I believe there will come a time, my child. There will come a time, and when it does, I hope you'll talk to me about it. I can't honestly say I'll understand how you feel, but I'll listen. I want to hear about it and work with you to change what you can, accept what you can't, and move on.

I've learned to do that myself. I had to, because your birth parents will always be important in my life, too, whether present or absent. Motherhood is different for me because I feel a profound sense of obligation to your birth mother. She sacrificed a part of herself in bringing you and me together, and I don't want to let her down. I want to be the mother she wished she could be. I want to be the mother you need me to be, and I want to be the mother I always hoped I could be. I want her choice to have been a good one, and I want you to grow up feeling grateful to your birth mother for making an adoption plan. I want both you and your birth mother to be glad that I'm your mother. I sure am.

Motherhood is different for me because of your birth father, because of what he meant to your birth mother and what he means to you. I'm often not sure what he means to you, but I know it's important. He's in your cells and your features and your thoughts, and that makes him important to both of us.

Mother's Day will always feel different for me than if you were my biological child. My joy at being your mother is mixed with thoughts of your birth mother, her loss of you, and her mother's loss of you, her biological grandchild. As I read and reread your tender handmade cards, I feel a little bit guilty. I'm acutely aware that I'm being celebrated for something I didn't do. Your birth mother did. I didn't make me a mother; she did. I doubt she celebrates that on Mother's Day.

Father's Day feels different for me because you were adopted. As we bake special treats for your father and make sentimental homemade gifts, I can't help but wonder what your birth father is doing. Adoption made your father a father and your birth father a birth father, and the difference between the two is starker on Father's Day than any other day of the year.

Your birthday, too, is different for me than it would be if you were my biological child. Your birth parents are present in every thought and conversation I have on your birthday, and I can't help feeling torn. I don't know if I want you to find a way to honor them in your celebration or claim it as your day, our day, our family's day. Maybe both. I don't want to thrust your birth parents into every experience or make you feel like you owe them a certain portion of your thoughts. You don't. Regardless of how we came to be, you are my child. But as your mother, I think of your first parents on your birthday, and I'm sure they think of you.

To my daughter

It seems strange now that for a long time I was afraid of having a daughter. I know a lot of women want nothing more, but I was never one of them. I didn't want the intensity of a mother-daughter relationship. Girls and their mothers—it's so complicated and intricate. I thought it was fragile. I thought it was too close. I was afraid I would mess it up, and even worse, mess my daughter up.

I was overwhelmed by the prospect of having to teach someone to be a girl, a female, a woman, who is comfortable in her own skin. Someone who trusts her own analysis, who likes what she sees in the mirror, and who can say no with confidence and without drama because she knows what she wants and she's not afraid of getting it. How would I teach a daughter to love her body without fixating her on physical appearance? How would I teach her to be kind and compassionate without making her into a people-pleaser who puts everyone's needs before her own? How would I teach her to be reasonably wary of boys and men without making her afraid? I would want my daughter to be strong but not aggressive, gentle but not weak, diligent but not a perfectionist, faith-filled but tolerant. I wondered how I would cultivate the mother-daughter closeness I assumed we should have without either of us losing ourselves in the process. I thought I would be a better mother to a boy.

I secretly panicked the first time I held you. *It's a girl after all. I have a daughter. A daughter! Very funny, God, now how do I do this?* I rarely panic anymore, and never about your gender. I know now what I couldn't know then, which is that I had to grow into our relationship as the relationship grew between us. I couldn't be your mother before I was your mother. I needed the experience of parenting you to shape me as your mother. I still do. I'm the mother I am today because of the daughter you are today and because of who we are together, and I'll be different tomorrow because you'll be different and the day will be different. I know now that I'll continue becoming your mother for the rest of my days, and rather than lose myself in the process, I'll find myself in new ways.

We were in the car, and I think you were three, the first time you said, "I wish Miss Teresa was my mother." As my heart collapsed, I felt my brain sizzle, and every ounce of air swooshed out of my lungs. I thought I was going to faint, or vomit, or faint into a pool of my own vomit. As I struggled to control the car, I caught your face in the rearview mirror. Sweet as ever, guileless, completely unaware of the chaos churning through my brain, you added, "I'll always love you, Mama, but I wish she was my mother." I knew you didn't mean what you said. I knew you meant you were fond of Miss Teresa and wanted to spend more time with her. I knew you meant it felt good to receive praise and encouragement from an adult outside our family. I knew it was a perfectly normal, benign childish fantasy, and I knew you weren't trying to hurt me. I cried anyway.

I cried tears from a place deep within myself that only exists because you are my daughter. I cried because I'll never be your biological mother, and maybe I'm not enough. I cried because I worry that someday you'll seek to understand your birth mother by getting pregnant before you're ready. I cried because I know some adoptees who try to get their birth mother's attention by starving themselves or shoplifting or driving drunk. I cried because I'm afraid that someday you'll say, "I wish so-and-so was my mother," and really mean it.

I can't imagine any mother loving her daughter more than I love you. I don't think it's possible. Many times I've thought my heart would burst with the joy of being your mother. Loving you is sometimes a challenge, usually a pleasure, and always an honor. My child, I know we belong together, and I'm so glad I'm your mother.

To my son
I always knew I wanted a son. People say that boys are easier to raise. Maybe so, but that's not why I wanted one. I liked the

idea of watching my son with his father. I liked the thought of teaching my son to value women. I looked forward to teaching my boy to understand them, respect them, and love them. I wanted to raise a man who could challenge women respectfully, compete against them honorably, and win and lose to them with grace. I assumed my son would be prewired for strength, assertiveness, confidence, and decision. I envisioned lovingly drawing out his natural gifts of humility, compassion, tolerance, and faith.

And yet, I secretly panicked the first time I held you. *It's a boy. I have a son. A son! I don't know the first thing about raising a boy!* I still panic on occasion, but never about your gender. I know now what I couldn't know then, which is that most of the time, you lead me. I learn how to raise you by raising you, by seeing what works and what doesn't, and by paying attention to the way you communicate with me. I learn how to make you into a man by loving your father. He is my role model for you.

I remember the first time you said you wanted to marry me. As my heart swelled, I felt lightheaded, and every ounce of humility deserted me. *Me? You want to marry me?* I knew you didn't mean what you said. I knew you meant you loved me and liked spending time with me. I knew you meant it felt good to think of yourself as tall and confident and important to me, like your father is. I knew it was a perfectly normal, benign childish fantasy, and I knew you would eventually come to your senses. I cried anyway.

I cried tears from a place deep within myself that only exists because you are my son. I cried because I'll never be your biological mother, and I hope that's OK. I cried because I know someday it might not be enough. I cried because I know you might seek a closer relationship with your birth mother, and I want it to go well for you. I cried because someday you'll say, "I want to marry you," and you won't be talking to me.

I can't imagine any mother loving her son more than I love you. I don't think it's possible. Many times I've thought my heart would burst with the joy of being your mother. Loving you is sometimes a challenge, usually a pleasure, and always an honor. My son, I know we belong together, and I'm so glad I'm your mother.

Chapter 6

I Want to Be Part of Your Process

Once upon a time I thought adoption was a wonderful thing. A real-life fairy tale of self-sacrifice and purest love. I used to think adoption was the story of single women too young, too poor, too addicted, or too emotionally immature to care for their babies. These women—noble-hearted, every one—loved their babies so much that they gifted them with the security and opportunity of "a real family" rather than sentence them to the certain suffering and dysfunction of a bastard's life.

In the adoption fairy tale, these unwed mothers found morally impeccable married couples whose hearts and homes brimmed with love and laughter, wisdom and warmth, whose lives were richly layered and complete but for one thing—a child to love and be family with. Adoption was the golden thread that bound these strangers together, weaving something unexpected, yet strong and beautiful, from the torn pieces in their lives. Neat and tidy, adoption was the quintessential happy ending for all.

I don't think that anymore. I can't. I've learned too much to ever again mistake adoption for a fairy tale. I know now that for some people, the experience is more like a Greek tragedy. I've met adoptees who are plagued by the perception that they were deliberately unchosen by their birth families, convinced that they were judged and found to be unsuitable before they had a chance to be anything at all.

I've met adoptees who say that although they love their adoptive parents and siblings, they have never felt deeply connected to them. I know adoptees who were never able to love their adoptive families, some of whom resent their adoptive parents for "denying the importance of biological connections" and forcing them to unlearn where they came from and who they really are. I know one who searched for her birth mother and, upon finding her, walked away from the only family she ever knew and moved in with the woman she considers her "real mother."

I've learned that adoption is *never* a fairy tale for birth mothers. It may be a plan, a solution, a best alternative ... a blessing, for some, but never a fairy tale. I've met women like Donna, who fled her boyfriend/abuser while pregnant with their second child. Although grateful that he "only" broke three ribs when he found her, she couldn't bear to subject another child to her life of fear and pursuit, so she made an adoption plan. Donna's son is now five years old, and she still regrets her choice. "I chose to give my son away rather than leave my abuser. What kind of a mother am I? How can I possibly defend that to my son or anyone else?"

I've met birth mothers who never *chose* adoption at all, women from the Baby Scoop Era (BSE)* who were forced into adoption by their doctors, ministers, social workers, and disgraced parents. Unwed and young (many of them teenagers), they were shamed, isolated, threatened, and coerced into surrendering their children. Many of them never even saw their babies, and almost without exception, the adoptions were completely closed. After their babies were taken from them (often just moments after birth), these mothers were systematically discarded, dumped back into their old lives with stern instructions to never talk about their "awful mistake" (the pregnancy, not the adoption). No one counseled these mothers about postpartum depression or post-separation grief. No one explained how their bodies were forever changed by pregnancy and childbirth. No one prepared them for the staggering depression, anxiety, and guilt they would feel. No one even acknowledged their loss. In fact, people acted as though these mothers should be grateful to the adoptive parents for agreeing to take on their dirty little secret.

What happened to millions of women and their babies during the BSE is almost incomprehensible today, but scorn for unwed mothers, and the assumption that they were universally unfit to parent, were widely accepted as professional opinion at the time. Consider these comments from BSE adoption professionals:

> "Unwed mothers should be punished and they should be punished by taking their children away." (Dr. Marion Hilliard of Women's College Hospital, *Daily Telegraph* [Toronto: November 1956])

> "Women having out-of-wedlock children tend to be rather disturbed people." (Jane Rowe, adoption social worker [1950–1970])

> "The caseworker must then be decisive, firm, and unswerving in her pursuit of a healthy solution for the girl's problem. The 'I'm going to help you by standing by while you work it through' approach will not do. What is expected from the worker is precisely what the child expected but did not get from her parents—a decisive 'No!' It is essential that the parent most involved, psychologically, in the daughter's pregnancy also be dealt with in a manner identical with the one suggested in dealing with the girl. Time is of the essence; the

maturation of the fetus proceeds at an inexorable pace. An ambivalent mother, interfering with her daughter's ability to arrive at the decision to surrender her child, must be dealt with as though she [the girls' mother] were a child herself." (Dr. Marcel Heiman, *Out-of-Wedlock Pregnancy in Adolescence* [1960], 71)

I have to specifically call your attention to this phrase in the last quote above: "An ambivalent mother, interfering with her daughter's ability to arrive at the decision to surrender her child." As if surrendering her child was the only acceptable course of action, as if it had already been decided, as if the baby's mother ought not to be allowed any sovereignty over her own life or that of the child she created.

No mother ever forgets her child, and to this day, many of the Baby Scoop Mothers live with the torment of having no idea what happened to their children. Some of them don't even know if they had a girl or a boy. It was the custom at the time to seal all adoption records, so these mothers have little or no information about the adoptive parents. These women live every day wondering if the children they gave birth to even know that they're adopted. Do they even know that they're loved by another mother? I can't imagine that pain. The pain of loving someone who may not know I exist. Perhaps the only thing worse would be wondering if the child I brought into the world is looking for me and can't find me. That's what life is like for some mothers from the BSE.

Today, there are birth mothers who don't see much difference between adoption during the BSE and adoption now. They believe the adoption industry manipulated them to make a buck, tore motherhood from their arms for money, for business, "for the good of the child." One such birth mother I know likens adoption to "having your heart carved out of your body with a letter opener and being told to get up, get out, and get on with your life. Just put this behind you."

I've met birth mothers who think people who adopt—people like me—are rich, selfish, callous, spoiled, evil. "Baby buyers." That's what they call us. As if we *purchased* their children. As if we emptied our savings to pay for the perverse thrill of shattering their lives. As if our decision to adopt is rooted in a twisted sense of self-entitlement. As if I think I deserve their children more than they do. I most definitely do not.

But sadly, I've learned that some adoptive parents *do* adopt by unethical or questionable means. Some adoptive parents *do* fit the profile of greedy, wealthy, judgmental baby-grabber. Some adoptive parents *do* hold themselves apart from and above "the kind of people who have children they don't want or can't afford." I'm sad to say that some adoptive parents make promises to birth parents that they never intend to keep. Some adoptive parents are so fixated on wanting to see themselves in their children or wanting to remake their children in their own image that they deny or denigrate the role of genetics in shaping who we are. Some adoptive parents are so busy feeling threatened by birth parents that they forget to feel grateful to them.

And yet I know adoptive parents who struggle mightily to connect with their adopted children. Adoptive parents who pour every ounce of their love and strength and energy into their children and find that it's nowhere near enough; there are some bonds that just won't be made. I know adoptive parents who fiercely defend their right to build a family through adoption, adoptive parents who can't imagine a deeper love than what they feel for their adopted child. I know adoptive parents who are acutely aware that one of the greatest joys of their lives was born of another mother's greatest pain.

Why am I telling you all this? Because it's part of the collective adoption experience, and you need to be aware of it. Because you and I and your father and your birth family are all affected by it. Because I want you to understand why some people think differently of adoption than you do. I want you to be clear about what is yours to deal with and what isn't. I want you to be able to separate your Self and your experiences from everyone else and theirs, including me and mine.

I've been surprised by the way my thoughts about adoption have changed, both in direction and degree, and I can't figure out why the more I learn, the less I know. Because my adoptive experiences have been positive and beautiful, I lived in a happy little adoption bubble for a long time. I was so caught up in my own adoptive experience that I naively thought it was fairly normative. I felt like an idiot when I first realized how wrong I was. *Of course adoption is wrenching, confusing, unsettling, and sad. How could I have missed that?*

I know now how I missed that. I missed it because your adoption was one of the most poignant, affirming, inclusive, and healing experiences of my life. *And* your birth family says the same thing. Yes, it was that way for them, too. Absolutely stellar.

I admit, I'm completely baffled by the adoption phenomenon. I believe to my core that I was meant to parent you, *exactly you*, but I can't explain the rest of it. I believe that you are a blessing, and I believe the cliché "everything happens the way it should," but I don't think your birth mother was predestined to become pregnant and adopt you out. I don't think she was chosen to suffer the loss of you so I could be your mother. I don't believe God shanghaied her sex life to provide me with a child. Like I said, I can't explain it. I'm just grateful for it.

The truth is that all adoptions create riddles. All adoptions are rooted in loss. All adoptions raise doubts and fears and dissatisfaction—with the process, with the system, with the waiting, with the questions, with the answers, with the searching, with the finding, and with our Selves. Yet, for me, and hopefully for you, adoption is a wonderful thing, warts and all. Not always, but mostly.

I want to be part of your process so I can remind you to look outside your own experience. I want you to see the beauty in adoption. I want you to celebrate the joy and marvel at the unexpected gifts that only adoption can bestow. I also want you to be more sensitive than I was to the fact that adoption fractures one family to make another. I want you to remember that adoption obligates people to dismantle intimate parts of their spirit, shed them, and walk away. I want to make you aware of injustice and abuse in the adoption industry. I want you to be angry about it and put yourself out there and work to fix it without losing sight of what's good about adoption.

I want to be part of your process so I can remind you to look *inside* your own experience. I want you to hold your history to the light, to see it for what it is and is not. I want you always to weigh your truth against everyone else's and remember that adoption brought you into your life. *This* life. *Your* life.

I want to be part of your process to make sure you are clear about the facts of your history, regardless of what anyone else's facts are. These are the facts:

> Your birth parents were not coerced into relinquishing.
>
> Your birth mother was not isolated, rejected, shamed, pressured, abandoned, or threatened while pregnant with you.
>
> She had options and support, your birth father, and a loving family around her.
>
> She imagined what your life would be like with her and without her.
>
> She imagined what her life would be like with you and without you.
>
> She questioned and deliberated and prayed, and ultimately, she chose adoption.

She chose us for you. Of her own volition, she opted out of mothering you. I can't honestly say why. I'm not her. I can only tell you what she has told me.

She loved you from the moment she knew about you.

She loves you still.

At the time you were born, she was not ready to be a mother.

She couldn't be the family she wanted you to have.

She has never regretted you. She regrets that when you were born, she wasn't at a place in her life where she could be your mom, but she's never regretted you coming into her life.

She's afraid you will think she let you down.

She thinks about you every single day.

We are an answer to her prayers.

She hopes you will understand.

You are forever in her heart.

It's easy to talk about the joy of adoption. Adoption builds families, makes parents and siblings, aunts, uncles, cousins, and grandparents. Adoption makes playmates and school friends, room mothers and den fathers. Adoption brings ballet tutus, baseball mitts, driveway chalk, bedtime stories, dinosaurs, prom dresses, scrapbooks, and memories into homes that otherwise wouldn't have them. Adoption sells greeting cards and magazines and headlines. Adoption renews faith. It gives hope. Adoption answers prayers and makes dreams come true. The joy of adoption is easy to see and talk about. It's parenthood like any other. Times a thousand.

The losses created by adoption can be stealthy. There is grief that may not have taken hold of you yet. Maybe it never will. But I want to help you recognize it in case it does. Adoption loss often masquerades as self-doubt, insecurity, depression, and hypersensitivity to being excluded or overlooked. If you feel chronically underappreciated, misunderstood, or wounded, you may be experiencing adoption-related loss.

Any significant beginning or ending in your life may trigger disproportional feelings of fear or loss or sadness. *Any significant beginning or ending*—becoming a teenager, starting at a new school, experiencing the breakup of a romantic relationship, turning eighteen, leaving home, graduating from college, losing your virginity, celebrating your birthday, getting married, having your own child, dealing with the death of a family member or friend—may bring different thoughts or feelings than you expected. You may not think it's related to adoption, and maybe it's not. But maybe it is. For a lot of people, it is.

Many women who were adopted as infants grow up feeling just fine about their birth mother's decision to relinquish but, years later, can't understand why they're not happier about getting pregnant, or why they struggle to bond with their babies. Holding their baby forces the first psychological confrontation with their birth mother and her decision to relinquish. Some women are overcome by the realization of how sweet and helpless their infant self was, and they are torn by rage toward their birth mother. One adult adoptee describes it this way:

> "I didn't think I had any unresolved feelings about being adopted, but when my daughter was born, I kind of fell apart for a while. I was terrified by her helplessness. Every time I looked

at her, I saw myself as a baby, and I realized I was just as helpless when I was adopted. For a while I was disgusted with my birth mother. I thought she must have been terribly cold or selfish to be able to walk out on me when I was so young. Gradually I got back to thinking of adoption as a decision she made about herself, not about me, but it took some time."

You, too, may struggle for balance as a parent. You may overreact to a perceived slight, or underreact to intense feelings. You may distance yourself or hover too close. You may personalize your child's failures and successes and feel them as your own. You may take responsibility for things that are your child's to deal with. Without realizing it, you may try to relate to your birth parents through your own children. You may cling too closely to your own child in a distorted effort to pay your birth parents back for abandoning you or to prove that they made a mistake in letting you go. You may find any rejection of your child almost unbearable. Even as you know, intellectually, that playmates argue and first crushes don't last, you may personalize these inevitable losses and make them about you and your birth parents. You may exhaust yourself trying to be the perfect parent, vowing that you will never miss an opportunity to support your child and never let them doubt your love, when in reality, it's likely that you will do both without meaning to.

You may find yourself feeling anxious or depressed when you expected to be deliriously happy. It's normal. It's all normal. You are normal. You are perfectly normal, perfectly You. By the way, do you have any idea how many non-adoptee parents do exactly these same things and feel these same feelings? In my unscientific estimate, close to 100 percent. All parents operate from the same home base—their own experience of being parented. All parents bring their unresolved issues into the relationship they have with their child. The key to parenting with clarity is to identify the source of your reaction and learn to parent in the present moment, not from the past.

One of the most important things I will do in my life is teach you to make the most of yours. Some adoptees waste precious years searching for balance and belonging because they don't realize that balance and belonging come from within. I want to be part of your process so I can be a counterweight when you need one. I hope you'll consider my perspective. I know you were the one adopted, but I was there, too.

You may be insatiably curious about the details of your birth. You might want to visit the hospital where you were born or the orphanage where you first lived, or drive through unfamiliar neighborhoods searching for anyone or anything that reminds you of someone or something you wish you could remember. You may think that Finding Yourself means digging for your past and rooting out your birth parents. This quote speaks to the universality of that drive:

> "Roles and relationships are not inseparable, either way around. Foster parents and stepparents are substitutes—mother and father figures—vital sometimes, and in some ways preferable, but never the same. Even adults who adopt infants and are the only parents they have ever known are still replacements for the parents they had but never knew. People will always want to know about their origins."[1]

It's natural and healthy to be curious about your birth family. Most of us want to know where we came from. I understand you wanting to know who gave you life, and when and why she left, and how she could do that, and where she is now. And who else made you? What does he look like, and why didn't he keep you?

Do they know where you are now? Have they tried to find you? Did they raise other children? Why them and not you?

In your mind, your birth parents can be anything you want them to be. They can be perfect. In your imagination, your birth parents say yes to the things I say no to. They understand everything and agree with all of your decisions and adore all of your friends. They think you're always right and that every word out of your mouth is brilliant as the sun. Their money grows on trees, their car keys are yours for the taking, their refrigerator is always full, they don't care what time you come in at night, and they never lose their tempers. They're flawless. In your imagination.

Imagination can make the prospect of reunion seem magical, like you're going to pull back the curtain in Oz and run headlong into the welcoming arms of a piece of yourself that's been missing from your life. Finally, someone who can reveal the secrets. Finally, someone who can answer all of your questions. Finally, someone who can fill in the gaps. Finally, someone who will give you that deep, organic sense of belonging that everyone but you seems to feel. You will see yourself in their faces. You will hear yourself in their voices. They will move like you, smile like you, *feel* like you. As your misty eyes meet, your whole being will vibrate, and you will share a profound sense of homecoming. Everything is perfect. In your imagination.

My child, because I love you, I hope your birth parents are everything you imagine them to be. And because I love you, I have to tell you that they may be far less. They are your *birth parents* because when you were born, they were not able to parent. Something in them or their life was out of balance … far enough out of balance that they couldn't be your family. For whatever reasons, they weren't able to take care of you in a healthy, loving, supportive way. Has that changed? Maybe. Maybe not. If they were very young when you were born, well, certainly, they've gotten older. If they were ill when you were born, hopefully they're well now. If they were poor or self-destructive, abused or addicted, they may still be. They may never be able to be with you the way you want them to be, not for a day, maybe not even for an hour

Although your birth parents are the only ones who can say for certain why they weren't able to raise you, I can tell you with absolute certainty that it wasn't about you. Your birth parents did not make an adoption plan because you weren't the right sex or the right color or the right baby. You were not left at the gate because you cried too much. They did not relinquish their rights because you weren't good enough or because you were too much trouble or because they didn't like you. Your birth parents made an adoption plan to give to you, not take away from you. They relinquished their rights because they wanted more for you than they were able to provide. They had the wisdom to know that the most loving decision they could make, the very most parental thing they could do, was to put your needs before their own. Ironically, that's the very thing they knew they couldn't do day in and day out, as parents must, but they were able to make that most important sacrifice for you, their child.

That brings me to a concern so many adoptees share with me in conversation—the question of being good enough. "Was I the child my parents hoped I would be when they adopted me? Have I been what they wanted?" In case you have any doubt, I'll tell you now. You are not at all the child I hoped you would be. You are not at all the child I wanted. You are much, much more. You far surpass my greatest hope. The reality of you leaves my dream of you in the dust … far behind … gasping for air. There is no way I could have imagined a child as wonderful as you. I'm honored to be part of your process, because I love you.

Sidebar

*Baby Scoop Era (BSE) refers to the period between 1945 and 1972 in the United States. The following excerpt is from the Baby Scoop Era™

Research Initiative (BSERI) Web site (http://www.babyscoopera.com):

The American Maternity Home Movement experienced radical change after 1945. Karen Wilson-Buterbaugh's research into the textbooks, papers, and conference presentations of social workers and sociologists of the Baby Scoop Era has revealed a movement in flux. Once the province of altruistic Christian women, the movement rapidly moved from a supportive model to a psychoanalytic model after WW II. Homes that had sheltered unmarried pregnant women, and trained them in the life skills they needed to successfully raise their children, began instead to promote closed, stranger adoption to married couples as the best social solution to the challenges presented by single motherhood. The change occurred as social workers began to practice within Maternity Homes, eventually pushing the Christian women out. The social work profession brought with it a psychoanalytic bias that informed their practice and radically altered the outcome of single pregnancy during this period. These practices persisted until 1972, a period of great social and technological change in the United States. After 1972, the number of domestic adoptions dropped dramatically.

After the early 1970s, easy availability of contraception, vastly increased economic and educational opportunities, and growing acceptance of single parenthood presented women with many more options then they had before. The years between 1945 and 1972, with its maternity reformatories, institutionally induced guilt, psychoanalytic explanations for single motherhood, and coercive adoption practices became a brief footnote in American social history, except to the cohort of women who survived these practices. These women carried into their adult lives unaddressed burdens of worry, pain and a corrosive secret. The effects of social work practice of these years are very much alive and well in the lives of millions of American women. These years are called the Baby Scoop Era, and these women, Baby Scoop Mothers.[2]

Chapter 7

I Think About Your Birth Parents

I think about your birth parents. Often. More often than I expected to, and probably more often than you realize. How could I not? They changed my life in a way that no one else could. Of all the people in the world, God chose them to create you and care for you before you were born. And they chose me. Of all the people in the world, they chose *me*. Wow.

Sometimes when I look at you, amazed that you're real and amazed that we're together, I get lost in the look of you. I get lost in the stories of your face. My mind wanders past the line of your jaw and the curve of your lips, past your birth parents, past your birth grandparents, through generations of immigrants and pioneers before them, and I wonder about those people who will always be part of you and never part of me. I wonder which of them handed down which part of you before you were born, before your birth parents were born, before I was born. I think about those people living their lives wherever they are and you living yours here ... a part apart. I think about them because you were of them before you were of me. They will always be the very beginning of who you are.

They are a beginning that you carry forward with you throughout the rest of your life. DNA keeps them present in you no matter how you adapt and evolve. I like that you have a part of them that no one else will ever have, and they have a part of you that no one else will know. Do they think of it that way? I wonder if your birth mother holds your birth in her mind as the beginning of a life apart or the end of a life together.

Sometimes I catch a shape of a name on a sound of a voice, or a flash of familiar on a tilt of a head, and just for a second, everything stops. Everything waits. Everything wonders. Is it her? Is that him? Is it? Is it? Then the voice shifts or the head turns, and it's just another stranger, just another someone doing something that has nothing to do with you or me or your birth parents, but I'm left with your birth parents on my mind. I'm left wondering how they are and what they're doing. I wonder if they're happy, healthy, kind, loved, content. I wonder if they're thinking about you. Thinking about us.

Sometimes I deliberately call them to mind, like on Mother's Day and Father's Day. *I'm a mother because of them. She's a birth mother because of me.* I wonder what Mother's Day means to her. Does she feel like she's your mother? Does anyone ask her about you or celebrate her as a mother? I wonder if she has other children, and if they give her the same kind of homemade cards you give me, and if, while holding one of their hand print paperweights or soup can bud vases, her mind wanders to you. I imagine it does. I imagine she misses you. I wonder if she feels in her bones how right her decision was. I hope she does. I sure do.

I knew we belonged together the moment I held you. "My child," I whispered. "I'm your mama," and you settled into my heart like it was your own. *Were there ever two people more perfect for each other?* As I trailed my finger gently across your feathery brows and your tiny pink lips, all sense of myself and my identity slipped away. Titles and labels—some of which I had spent years earning, had labored, sacrificed, and even competed for—slid like greased piglets off my shoulders and out of my mind. *I'm a mother now. A* mother. *A mother is what I am, Mother is who I am, motherly is how I am, in the motherhood is where I am. You made me a mother, Little One. You did what science and medicine did not.* And I thought about her.

Did she hold you like this? Did she love you this much? Did you feel her arm beneath your warm little head, feel her heart beating next to yours ... feel her breath on your cheek? Did her tears fall on you as mine do now? Already I can't remember time before you. Already I can't imagine you gone. Already I can't imagine looking in your eyes and knowing it's the last time. Already I can't imagine walking away. How did she do it?

For almost a year, your birth mother carried you everywhere she went. She wondered about you. She worried about you. She talked to you and fed you and felt you move. She made plans for you. She loved you. She made space in her body for you to grow. She gave you her voice, her thoughts, her movement, her sleep. She gave you breath and life. She gave you everything she could, and when her time to give to you was finished, she gave you to me.

She wished she could keep you. She wished she could raise you. She wished she could give you joy and discovery and security and health, confidence and opportunity and wisdom and peace, but she knew she couldn't. She knew she didn't have the maturity or consistency or support to create the life she wanted you to live. She wanted you to be able to plan a future and have the means to pursue your dreams. She wanted you to belong to a strong, healthy, joyful family. She wanted you to have parents who could be everything she wished she could be for you. And so she did what all good mothers do. She gave you what you needed. She gave you me.

I wonder what her life has been like since the last time she saw you. Did she wake up the next morning and forget, just for a moment, that you were gone? And remembering, and knowing that she gave you everything she could, did she grieve anyway? Did her heart ache for you? I imagine it did, because the best decisions are often the most painful, especially for mothers.

I imagine she cried for the loss of you—cried for the loss of what might have been and who you might have become. Some people say they don't understand how a mother can place her child for adoption. They say they don't understand how a mother can entrust her child to someone else, knowing she may never see that child again. I don't believe them. I think they do understand. I think they understand exactly the wrenching, searing pain of not being able to take care of your own child. I think they understand exactly the visceral fear of not being enough. I think they understand exactly the terms of sacrifice adoption requires. I think they are awed and humbled by your birth mother's decision, and they doubt they have courage enough to do what she did. I'm almost certain I don't.

More than anything, your birth mother wanted for you what every mother wants for her child—for you to know how very much she loves you. She wanted you to know it every minute of every hour of every day for the rest of your life, and so she took care of you in the best way she knew how. She loved you enough to release you into the life you were meant to have. She loved you enough to recognize that I should be your mother, and you should be my child. She knew that I would love you enough for two mothers, or two hundred, or two million … as many as you would need.

Adoption is usually thought of in terms of surrendering a child, but when birth parents place a child for adoption, they also surrender a part of themselves and their future. They surrender who they might have become as parents. They surrender a life that might have been. They surrender the family you might have become together. Your birth mother's life would be very different if she were able to be your mother, and she herself would be very different from the person she is now. Parenthood has changed me in ways I couldn't have anticipated. I have to think it would have changed your birth mother, too. I wonder if she thinks about that. Is she curious about what you might have become together? Does she imagine what she would be like as your mother? Do you? You surprise me in so many ways, and your presence changes me every day. I wonder how your absence changes her. I wonder how her absence changes you.

It's been an honor and a thrill to watch you grow into your own Self, a person so very different from the baby your birth parents knew, so very different from the baby we brought home. Yet your essence is the same. I can still see the earliest You in the person you are today, and that makes me think of your birth parents.

I think about your birth father. Was he there when you were born? (So many aren't.) Did he recognize himself in your tiny face? Did he give you his name? I wonder if he held you, talked to you, kissed you goodbye. Did he whisper that he loved you? I wonder if any of his family or friends knew that his child had been born. Biology cuts both ways for birth fathers. With no outward sign of his paternity, your birth father may have simply walked away. And with no outward sign of his paternity, your birth mother may have simply withheld the fact that they had conceived. Assuming that he knew about you, your birth father had different decisions to make than your birth mother had. He may have disagreed with her about making an adoption plan or he may have chosen to work with her on it. He may have told his family and friends about you or he may not have told anyone. He may have wanted nothing to do with your birth mother's pregnancy. He may have wanted to be far more involved than your birth mother was willing to accept.

When I think about your birth father, it's with a touch of sadness. I wish I knew more about him. I wish I could give you more. He is as important a part of your beginning as your birth mother is, although you'll find many people who disagree with me on that point. Regardless of what he said and did, or didn't say and didn't do, he is your first father. He created you, and I will always be grateful to him for that. I hope you will be, too.

I think some things about your birth parents that are difficult to think. I'd like to know if they had other children after you, and if they had them with each other or someone else. I wonder if they're parenting any of them. I wonder if these siblings of yours know about you. What do they understand about you and me and why your life is here and not there? What do you understand about that? I wonder if your birth parents talk to each other about you. I wonder how they feel about each other now.

I think about your birth parents and I wonder about the details of their lives. Sometimes when I see you absorbed in a book or music, I wonder if they're doing the same thing right now. I love to notice the things about you that are like them and different from me. I get a glimpse into your deepest self, where the indeliberate and indelible parts of your personality reside. When I notice those things, I'm reminded that you and I are part of a larger whole, a whole that includes your birth parents and your extended biological family. And whether or not you have contact with them, you and they and I will always share the unique circle of your life.

Mostly I wonder what your birth parents think about you. Do they miss you? Do they imagine what you look like now? Are they curious about your favorite color and what you eat for lunch? I hope they think of you on your birthday. I want your presence in the world to be important to them. I used to fantasize about them celebrating each year on the day they brought you into being and into my life. I imagined them walking around on your birthday in a happy glow, knowing they gave you a better life and gave a childless couple a chance to have a family. I know better now. I've talked with enough birth mothers to realize that your birthday probably falls somewhere between a root canal and a poke in the eye with a sharp stick for your birth mother, and maybe your birth father. I especially think about your birth mother, and I wonder if she cries on your birthday. I know I would. Heck, I do!

No matter how many people tell her she did the best thing for you, and no matter how deeply she knows they're right, it's never easy to lose someone you love. I hope she finds some peace in knowing that I hold her loss very close to my heart, for her greatest loss is my greatest gain, and I will always be grateful to her for trusting me.

Do your birth parents ever see a child with eyes or a nose or a smile that reminds them of their own and think, *Could that be* … ? If we bumped into them someday, somewhere, would they know who you are? Do they tell people about you? What do they say?

Do your birth parents wonder how you are like or not like them? I do. Some things about you are so much like me, and others are so different. Your laugh, your temperament, your face when you concentrate—who is that? I wonder if your birth mother tosses her head like you do, or if your birth father moves just that way. I wonder what you got from them and what you got from me.

Do they wonder if I let you have a cell phone or make you wear a bike helmet? Do they wonder if I opened a college fund? I want them to know that I've taught you to be respectful, to wash your hands before you eat, and to call if you're going to be late. I want them to know that we say our prayers together every night before bed. I want them to know that I'm doing my best to make you a citizen of your history as well as of your present, that I look for opportunities to expose you to your roots, to surround you with the language, music, colors, faces, and food that you first knew.

I think about your birth parents when people say you look like me or laugh like me or you're stubborn like me. I sometimes tire of having to decide what to disclose, and when, and how much, and to whom. I don't like feeling as if I have to defend your birth parents when people find out that you were adopted or reassure the people who apologize for not knowing. "Actually, she looks a lot like her birth mother," I say, and they look confused and then hastily whisper, "I'm sorry. I didn't *know*," leaving me to either reassure them that no apology is necessary and there is no reason they would have known, or to say nothing and, by my silence, comply with the idea that there is something they should be sorry for. "Adoption isn't a secret handicap," I sometimes say. "It's the way our family came together."

I think about your birth parents when I tell you that children are created within marriage, by a woman and a man who love each other very much and decide they want to share their love with children. We both know by now that's not entirely true. If it were, I wouldn't be your mother; your birth mother would. When I tell you that your body may be ready for sex before your emotions and spirit can appreciate the level of intimacy and commitment sex is meant to express, I think about your birth parents. I'm not sure how to be respectful of them without implicitly condoning teen sex and pregnancy. On the one hand, I caution you against risking the creation of a life you're not ready to support, and on the other hand, I tell you that your birth (to your unwed birth parents) is a blessing to me. The best I've come up with is to point out that your birth parents set themselves up to have to make some very difficult decisions, and they will live with the ramifications for the rest of their lives. Why deliberately set yourself up for the possibility (probability?) of that kind of heartache?

I think about your birth parents when I hand you the car keys and remind you to be careful, because I think I might die if I lost you. I love you so much, and I can't imagine not seeing you or hearing your voice anymore. What is it like for them?

I think of your birth parents when I know you're struggling with your own questions and mixed feelings about them and your roots. I think of them and I wish they had been more careful, if only to have spared you this struggle.

Sometimes I don't think about your birth parents. Our hearts are so integrated (yours and mine) that I almost forget that we're an adoptive family. I just don't think about it. In fact, I'm sometimes startled when other people mention it. At times I don't think about your birth parents because I don't want to be reminded of your native bond with another mother. You are forever linked to her in a relationship that doesn't include me. I know that sounds childish … I'm not proud of feeling selfish, but I do feel it from time to time. I searched and waited and prayed to find you. Are you waiting and praying to find her? If you find her, will you want to meet her? If you meet her, will you want a relationship with her? And then what? And then … what? That's why I don't think about your birth parents. I waited so long to find you, and there's a part of me that's afraid I might lose you. Not a big part, but a part, nonetheless.

Sometimes I choose not to think of them because I'm uncomfortable about something I know of them. I may know more about your birth parents than I have shared with you. Certainly, you have a right to know your own history, but as your parent, I have an obligation and an interest in revealing it to you in the right way at the right time. Your birth parents granted me that responsibility through adoption. Some truths require specific context, and I owe it to all of us to wait for the right context to develop.

I wonder if your birth parents think about me. If I were a birth mother, I would. I would be curious about the temperament of the adoptive family and the routines of their daily life. I would wonder if the adoptive parents talk about me and, if so, what they say. I want your birth parents to know that you are the center of my life. I want them to know they made me a better parent. They deepened my understanding of love and they gifted me with a profound partnership that I will never take for granted. I hope they know that we only speak of them with respect and admiration, and that we are forever grateful to them. I want them to know that you are as much my child as if you came from my body and that your heart and your spirit are at home here with mine. I want them to know that I think of them with love.

Chapter 8

You Are Responsible for You

Some people will tell you that when you were adopted, you suffered a profound primal loss. They will tell you that as a result of that loss, you harbor shame you may not even be aware of, that you were irreparably traumatized when your birth mother severed her native bond with you, and as a result, you will never be able to fully trust anyone. They will tell you that buried deep in your subconscious is the conviction that you are innately unlovable and that this subconscious belief keeps you from really loving yourself or anyone else. These people—some of whom call themselves "adoption experts"—who have never met you, never spoken to you, and have likely never even heard of you, claim to know you better than you know yourself. You were adopted, and they think that's all they need to know.

Well, they're wrong. Wrong, wrong, wrong. They're wrong when they assign power to your loss, they're wrong when they say the trauma is irreparable, and they're wrong when they think "adopted" is all they need to know about you. Separation and loss are neither innately powerful nor irreparable; they are universal and ultimately impotent. Everyone separates. Everyone loses. Everyone chooses to either actively heal and grow or fester and live in pain. Everyone does it differently, but in all cases, we define the experience; it doesn't define us.

Separation and loss break early into our awareness. We are separated with the cutting of the umbilical cord, suddenly and literally cut off from our life source without our consent. Our primal bond is severed by force, and we are fully disconnected from the only life we've known. We are lost from our mother's body, and our mother is lost to us. Dramatic? Yes. Tragic? No. It's not tragic because we are organically prepared for the separation. We are naturally equipped to compensate for the loss of physical closeness. We are born cute and sweet because humans are drawn to cute, sweet little creatures. We are born knowing how to cry so we can summon others to us when we want them close. We are born with the urge to suck so we will be drawn near and fed. We reflexively curl our fingers tenderly around the hands that hold us so we can feel secure. Just moments old, we begin to compensate for our loss.

Separated from our mother, we are joined again through feeding, holding, gazing, stroking, and affection. We separate and we join, we lose and we gain. We sever and we attach. We push and we pull in order to grow forward in our lives. We leave behind to move ahead. That's our nature.

Our first separation doesn't slice at the depths of who we are. In fact, it cuts us free to become who we might. It doesn't create psychic scar tissue for us to heal around; it allows us to realize the fullness of our psychic potential. Rather than surviving in spite of the cut, we exist *because* of it. We cannot become individual until we *are* individual. We cannot think and feel and experience our own lives until they are our own. The internal bond must break to give life to the external being. We separate because we must. We separate to survive.

The drive for separation that begins at birth continues through childhood, adulthood, and to the end of life. As toddlers we individuate from our parents, rabidly protesting any attempt to curtail our independence. As adolescents we fervently assert our independence from all forms of authority. We reject those closest to us, our family, in dogged pursuit of recognition as Individual Self. We eventually separate physically as well as emotionally, leaving home to create a new home, leaving schools and teams and clubs and friends. We leave jobs for better opportunities and one neighborhood for another, and through our lives, we leave a trail of severed relationships that leads all the way back to our pre-birth. Why are we able to heal from the loss of a friendship or the death of a family member? Why are we able to function post-breakup or divorce? Because we can heal … if we choose to.

Consider a mother who miscarries, or parents whose child dies. An intimate biological bond is ruptured without consent. They are separated. They have lost. They grieve. And yet they go on. They go on to other days, other relationships, maybe other children; they go on to join and lose again and again. They go on because they decide to. They go on because they make the decision to heal from separation. They make the decision to live fully after the loss. Your primal separation may be painful and profound and may cut to the bone, but you can make the decision to heal. You can choose to flourish right where you are. Starting now. You are responsible for you.

There is no shortage of expert opinion promoting the "adoptee as victim" perspective. There are plenty of people who see adoption as a handicap. They want you to believe that your first separation sentenced you to a lifetime of deficiency, insecurity, and self-hatred, and that no matter how hard you try, you'll never escape your predestined dysfunction.

Don't you believe it. Don't you believe it for one minute. You were not born into a preordained set of feelings or crises. No one is. There is no such thing as *congenital loss* or *congenital alienation*. How can it be that your first separation maimed your spirit so deeply that all of the love and nurturing and security and bonding you experience afterward leave you empty and unfulfilled? How can it be that of all the pain and loss you experience in a lifetime, most of which you are far more aware of—and perhaps share responsibility for—adoption is the singular injury that cannot be healed? It doesn't make any sense. Do you really believe that your first hours or days or even months determine the direction of the rest of your life? Do you really believe that since your birth parents were unable to parent well, you will never be whole? Do you really believe that one decision set your life on an unalterable course? I don't. It's completely illogical, and I love you too much to let you think that way. I love you too much to let you buy into the myth of the adoption legacy.

You are not simply an outcome of your birth parents' decision; you are an amalgam of every experience you've ever had. Since you came into being, you have been collecting information, reacting instinctively, and responding deliberately to sights, sounds, smells, tastes, and textures. Each day of your life, you have observed, engaged, and evaluated the people and the world around you, forming impressions and making decisions. You have felt pain, fear, separation, and loss in a variety of circumstances, and you have absorbed it, learned from it, and become stronger because of it. The decisions you make are much more powerful in your life than any decision your birth parents made.

I was separated from my mother and lost in a store when I was three, but I shop freely today. I burned my hand on the stove as a child, yet I cook dinner almost every night. My high school sweetheart dumped me for my best friend, and I lived to make new friends and love other boyfriends. I've learned to change what I can and work around the rest. You can do the same. Of course you will hurt sometimes. We all do. But you can move on if you choose to.

You are not a victim of adoption anymore than you are a victim of your gender, skin color, height, weight, accent, personality, race, or culture of origin. Adoption matters as much or as little in your life as you decide it does. You were born into this life because it is yours, and you came into it exactly as you should. This life of yours is fully ripe; it's up to you to pluck every opportunity for discovery, joy, and growth. I want you to look back someday on your life well-lived and be pleased with the history you created. The relationships, the events, the triumphs, and the failures—all of the particulars are yours.

Adoption may be the most significant, most intimate, most life-altering event in your life that isn't about you. Think about it. It's about your birth parents. It's about who they were and where they were in their lives at the time you were born. It's about their emotional maturity (or immaturity), their financial stability (or instability), and their relationship with each other. It's about your birth mother not wanting to leave you in day care twelve hours a day while she goes to college part-time and works full-time to feed you and herself enough that she has the strength to get up the next day and do it all over again. It's about your birth family making the heartbreaking decision that they simply cannot give you the basic necessities—adequate food, clean water, secure shelter, qualified medical care—that everyone needs and deserves. You were adopted, but the decision to make that happen wasn't about you. It was about the circumstances of your birth parents when you were born.

If you let the fact that you were adopted direct your life, that *is* about you—not about your birth parents or me or anyone else. You take responsibility for that. Although your birth parents made the first decision in your life, you are responsible for the decisions and choices you make now. The choices you have today are born of the choices your birth parents made. It's always that way, adoption or not. All children are bound in some way to the decisions of those who came before them. Your birth parents made their choices. You make yours.

Some adoptees persist in thinking of adoption as a complete rejection by their birth parents. They think that if they had somehow been irresistible, their birth parents would have "kept" them. Some adoptees refuse to let themselves fully experience the joyous blessings of a family formed through adoption, choosing instead to frame their experience on an obsessive foundation of first being unchosen by their birth parents. I hope you recognize that as self-indulgent and self-defeating. Of course you didn't do anything to cause yourself to be adopted. There is nothing you could have or should have said or done differently. How could there be? You were a baby ... a child ... no more able to alienate your first parents than you were able to perform brain surgery. Your birth parents didn't reject *you*. They rejected the role of parents. It was about them, not you.

If you accept that adoption has the power to make a mess of your life, you must also accept that it has the power to make a masterpiece of it. That's right. If you believe adoption has the power to destroy you, you must also believe it has the power to elevate you. Think about it. If you impart power to something— in this case, the power to determine the course of your life— you surrender control. You don't get to direct the power. So if adoption has the power to make your life worse, it can also make it better. The odds are fifty-fifty both ways. You're just as likely to be elevated by adoption as you are to be defeated by it. Your life as an adoptee is a total crapshoot. Pure chance. You are completely at the mercy of this thing called adoption. Is that really what you believe?

Has it ever occurred to you to pin your successes on adoption? Have you ever thought of crediting adoption for everything that's *right* in your life? No? Why not? If all of your problems can be traced to the fact that you were adopted, then by rights, all of your achievements and everything you've accomplished can also be traced to the fact that you were adopted. That means you can't take credit for ... well, for anything that's right in your life. You don't deserve a pat on the back for anything you've accomplished. Your birth parents do. They're the ones who set you on this path. They made it possible for you to be adopted, which set you up for a life of success, right?

You see, you can't have it both ways. You can't pin all of what's wrong on adoption and all of what's right on yourself. That's like blaming the fast-food industry for making you fat, then giving yourself credit for taking the weight off. Fat or fit, it's all you. You're either responsible for what you put in your mouth or you're not. A+ or D–, you're either responsible for your grades or you're not. Get fired or get promoted, you're either responsible for your job performance or you're not. You can't blame your teacher if you fail and your boss if you get fired, but credit yourself for making honor roll or getting a promotion. Good, bad, successes, and failures, you are responsible for you.

I know you didn't choose to be adopted. I know you didn't choose to leave your first mother. I know you didn't choose to be my child. Well, guess what? I didn't choose the circumstances of my birth either. I didn't choose my parents or my siblings or my life, and I don't know anyone who did. You can't choose your past, but you can choose to accept that your birth parents loved you as well as they could. You can choose to realize that they made an adoption plan to give you more, not to leave you with less. You can choose to understand that "what lies behind us and what lies before us are tiny matters compared to what lies within us." You can choose to integrate the pain of the past with the strength of the present and the opportunity of the future and move on. Or you can choose to cultivate anger and pain and resentment. You can choose to completely reject the notion of personal responsibility and spend your life blaming other people for what ails you. Yes, you can do that, but it won't change the truth, and it won't make anything better. And it won't hurt anyone else as much as it hurts you—not me, not your birth parents, not anyone.

Every experience changes you. Every day leaves you different. You are responsible for the *way* you change. You are responsible for moving yourself in a positive direction. Be suspicious of "victim" labels. They drain your energy and solve nothing. Resist all temptation to pluck adoption or any other event from your past and call it the Defining Moment. The only moments that define you are those you inhabit, those you grab hold of … feed on … and make your own.

Certainly, adoption alters the course of your life. Certainly, adoption presents you with unique challenges. So does being born with above- or below-average intelligence. So does being born into a large family or an athletic family or a famous family. So does physical beauty or the death of a parent. Everything about you alters the course of your life. Your life is different if you are a firstborn Asian male than it would be if you were a last-born Italian female. Your life is different if you are born into Christianity rather than Buddhism. Your life is different if your parents are educated or alcoholic or vegetarian or deaf. Everything about you alters the course of your life, but no single thing defines it. It's up to you to decide what adoption means to you and where it fits in your personhood. Is adoption a page in your birth story, an event in your past, the means by which you were joined with your family? Or is it a lingering emotional abscess? Is it a rejection of you by your first mother? Is adoption an end or a beginning? You decide.

Your birth parents loved you. They chose to give you life. They gave you *life*. And they gave you adoption. Were they hurt by the adoption? Definitely. Did they know it would hurt you? Maybe, but they didn't hurt you intentionally. Their intention was to provide for you as well as they could, and they believed adoption was the way to do that. Some people argue that adoption fails miserably in that regard, and for some people, it does. Some people say that birth parents choose adoption because they lack the support necessary to make a different choice, and some do. Some people mock the phrase "Your birth parents made an adoption plan because they love you." They say that mothers don't "give their children away" because they love them. Of course they don't. Adoption isn't the expression of their love; adoption is a testament to it. Adoption shows the strength of their love. Only a mother who truly loves her child can choose to put the child's needs before her own. Only a mother who truly loves her child can choose a life apart because she believes it is better for her child. Only a mother who truly loves her child is willing to live with the loss for the rest of her life in order to give her child a more balanced, secure, fulfilling life.

As your parent, I have made decisions that hurt me. I have made decisions that hurt you. I may have chosen a course of action because I lacked the support necessary to choose a different one. But it was my decision to make. Since I brought you home, I have always made decisions with your best interest in mind. I hope you know that your birth parents did the same.

Blaming adoption for what's wrong in your life is weak and cowardly. Don't blame anyone else for what challenges you. When you struggle, when you hurt, when you're lost or bored or angry, take responsibility for yourself. Care enough about yourself to improve your situation, and understand that the only way to change your situation is to change yourself. You can't change *anyone* but yourself. You can cry and you can storm and you can drink, drug, and cut yourself ... and guess what? The world will keep turning. Everyone around you will continue being who they are. Everything that has happened in your life will still have happened. Your birth mother is not going to come looking for you because you starve yourself. You're not going to prove your worth by having sex with a lot of people. Drama will not make you matter more. And whatever pain you're trying to numb will be waiting for you when the buzz wears off. If you plan to spend the rest of your life running away from part of yourself, let me save you the trouble. You're not going to make it. You will wear out long before the pain does. The only way to change your life is to change yourself. Starting right now.

I don't expect you to handle everything with grace and precision. I don't expect you to figure everything out on your own. I don't want you to hide your need for support or clarity or encouragement or a good, cleansing cry. Taking responsibility for yourself doesn't mean you have to handle everything alone. It means recognizing that where you came from isn't nearly as important as where you're going and how you're going to get there. It means acknowledging that you have a new opportunity every day to create the life you want. You have a new opportunity every day to direct yourself toward your goals, and I know you can achieve great things. Even if you're bugged, after all this time, that your birth parents made decisions that altered your life, you alone have the power to direct your life from this point forward. You alone decide what to do with today.

Part of personal responsibility is taking good care of yourself physically, mentally, emotionally, and spiritually. That includes asking for help when you need it and doing the work necessary to regain your balance. Respect your body's need to move and stretch and be strengthened. Breathe deeply. Break a sweat.

You are responsible for your identity and your self-image. It's up to you to do things you can be proud of. It's up to you to decide who you want to be and then be that person. Feed yourself with food and friends that nourish you. Recognize when you need other people, and ask them to be with you. Understand that you may struggle to balance yourself in the face of real or perceived rejection. Some adoptees say that even small losses feel huge to them, and even minor slights cause disproportional psychic or emotional distress. Although I don't believe that your feelings today are caused by an adoption in your past, your feelings are nonetheless vivid and valid. They are yours. They are real. I respect that.

Throughout your life, you will do either more or less than you think you are capable of, simply by deciding to. Every decision you make will move you either closer to or farther away from your goals. Adoption was a decision your birth parents made about their life, and a decision I made about mine, and although you were at the center of both decisions, adoption has absolutely no bearing on what you do with your life. You are neither limited nor liberated by your genetics. You have no more or less opportunities or abilities than anyone else. You are capable of managing your life ethically, productively, and happily, and I expect you to do so. I expect a lot from you because I know you, and I know what you can do.

There is no one else in the world exactly like you; there never was before and there never will be again. Only you. You have an awesome responsibility: to join yourself with a world in progress and make it better for your being here. No one else can do what you can. No one else has had your experiences. No one else is a product of your unique history. Everything that has happened to you, for you, around you, by you, makes you who you are. I treasure you because you are completely unique.

You know that a caterpillar changes into a butterfly, but do you really know *how*? Do you know that in order to advance to the next phase of its life, the caterpillar must change everything vital about itself? While in the chrysalis, its entire physical being—the only life-form it has ever known—completely liquefies and becomes something different. The caterpillar loses itself. Nothing familiar remains as the creature, now a butterfly, beats its wings against the walls of the cocoon. Beating, beating, beating, it seeks much more than simple escape, for the butterfly knows instinctively what we must learn through experience. The butterfly knows that in order to develop fully, it must beat its wings again and again. The beating builds strength and coordination, and must be done within the safety of the cocoon. It is only through this struggle that the butterfly is able to emerge strong and vibrant enough to fly and survive.

There is a parable about a young boy who watched a butterfly beat its wings against the walls of its cocoon. After a while, the boy could no longer bear to watch the creature struggle, so he gently tore a hole in the cocoon for the butterfly to crawl out. The boy watched in sorrow as the damp, limp butterfly died in his hand without ever so much as stretching its wings. The boy's attempt to rescue the butterfly destroyed the creature's only chance of survival by taking away the butterfly's opportunity to grow strong. The boy wanted to help, but he didn't know what the butterfly needed. He only knew what *he* would need, and he acted from that perspective. He took responsibility for the butterfly that it needed to take for itself.

There will be people in your life who are like that boy. There will be people in your life who will try to help by rescuing you from yourself. Remember the butterfly. Don't let anyone take responsibility for you that you need to take for yourself. Don't wait for someone else to fix you, and if anyone tries, tell them to back off. Take every opportunity to grow strong. Believe that you are worth your own struggle. Believe that you are worth the effort. Believe that you will emerge strong and beautiful and free. And you will.

You can be everything you want to be, because you have a life and people who love you. You have been loved from your very beginning. You have every opportunity to become who you want to be.

Chapter 9

Before You Search

> Children carry in their souls the early knowledge of not being chosen by their birth parents. Throughout their lives they reach for connections—for people who look like them, for the people who gave them life.
>
> —Kathy Lancaster, *Keys to Parenting an Adopted Child*

If you decide the journey to your beginning is one you must make, I hope you talk to me before you set out. Don't worry, I'm not going to try to talk you out of it. I'm not hurt by your decision, and I'm not afraid of your search. What I *am* afraid of is you shutting me out or thinking you have to search in secret. Too many adoptees do. *You don't.* Your drive to find your roots doesn't make me question your loyalty or your love. You are my child, unconditionally and forever. Nothing can change that. I'm not in competition with your birth mother, and I know how much you love me.

I want you to include me so I can remind you to be careful. Search and reunion can be confusing and painful, and I'd like to help you take care of yourself. I want you to include me so I can be happy with you if you find things that make you happy. I want you to include me because I'm curious. I'm curious to know what you find and even more curious about what you're looking for. What exactly are you hoping to discover? How do you think it will make your life different or better or more meaningful? I'm interested because I love you and because anything you bring into your life also touches mine.

Your birth parents have shaped both of us, albeit in different ways. They expanded my world. They taught me things no one else could about love and sacrifice and openness of heart. They enlarged my understanding of grace and the power of acceptance. They gave me you. No one else could have done that. Your birth parents shaped the core of who you are. Your genes are their genes, your blood is their blood, the essence of who you are begins with them. The prospect of reunion with them may symbolize identity, truth, resolution, belonging, closure, or certainty, and possibility pulls you like a magnet toward what you think you want. But sometimes what you want turns out to be entirely different from what you thought you wanted, and you won't know that until it's too late. You can't unlearn something you've learned; you can't un-experience anything. Being ready to search means much more than having a desire for information, and I'd like to talk with you about that. I'd like to help you stay clear about why you're searching and what to do with what you find.

The first thing you need to do is get real. Your history is real, your birth parents are real, and their feelings are real. Any contact between you will make them forever real to you. Your birth parents have built real lives and real relationships with real people; they may have had other real children, whose lives and feelings are as real as your own. What they think and what they want will become as real as what you think and want, and there will be no way to make any of it unreal afterward. Have you thought about what that will be like? Have you considered the psychological and emotional burden that comes with knowing them as real people? It's easy to make plans and retain boundaries when you're talking to yourself or to me about a possible reunion, because it's abstract … it's hypothetical. But it will be much more complicated once your birth parents are "real."

In the space of a few moments, you will form impressions, both positive and negative, that will remain real to you and be difficult to change. I know one adoptee who reunited with her birth mother after waiting twelve years to search and then searching for three. She says she realized within the first half hour that the meeting had been a huge mistake:

> "I had built her up in my mind as something like a perfect older sister. I thought she would look like me and understand me. I thought I would finally feel like I found someone who was part of me. It was a terrible disappointment. We were completely different, and not only that, she acted like she couldn't care less, like she only met with me out of obligation. I wish it never happened. Now when I think of her, that's all I see … someone who couldn't care less that I exist. I wish I never knew that."

It's important to mourn what you've lost before you search. You need to be clear about what you can expect to find and what you will never have. You do not have your birth family as your family. Even if you find them, they will not be your family. They will always be your biological parents; they will not be your family. Your birth parents are not who they were when they placed you for adoption. They will never again be those people. How could they be? They have lived as many days since then as you have. Day after day they have evolved and changed, won and lost, given and taken, just as you have. No one stays the same, and the time for them to parent the infant You has passed. It's gone forever. It will never be. If you think you know what (and who) you're missing, you need to let go of that, because your birth parents will not be what you're missing. They will not be who you want them to be. They will be who they are now, independent of you, and it's an injustice to everyone if you proceed without being ready to embrace them as they are now.

Similarly, you are who you are now, independent of your birth parents. It was painful for them to say goodbye to you, and they may not have let go of their image of you as you were the last time they saw you. They may not be able to embrace who you are now. They may struggle to see you as my child, a vital part of our family. They may feel wounded by our bond. Is that yours to deal with? Yes and no. You're not responsible for their feelings, but you will bear responsibility for bringing yourself into their present tense. Are you committed to doing so with sensitivity and respect for them, regardless of how they receive you? I hope you will consider that before you search. I think you owe them that.

If you're able to locate your birth parents, you may feel like you finally found something very important, only to find them angry at you for invading their privacy and disrupting their lives. They may pretend not to remember your birthday. They may actually not remember. They may want to pretend you don't exist. Are you ready for that possibility? If it happens, will you be able to understand it as being about them and not about you? Your birth parents may be alcoholic. Drug addicted. Pregnant. They may cry and ask you for money. They may blame you for everything that's wrong in their lives. They may say things about me that hurt or confuse you. I say this not to denigrate your birth parents, but to prepare you for their humanity. They're human. They're as imperfect as I am and you are. They are not any ideal you carry in your mind. The decision to make an adoption plan was probably one of the most painful decisions they've ever made, and sometimes the only way to move past pain is to deny it. Your birth parents may have had to disguise their pain as anger or apathy in order to heal from the loss of you. Your birth parents deserve to grieve their adoption losses in their own way, on their own time line. You may not like what you find out about your birth parents or what they have to say, and I'd like to help you prepare yourself for that.

Have you considered that your birth parents might not be able to answer your questions? They might not remember some of the details you want. You may ask your birth mother something about your birth father that's terribly important to you to know, and she may not remember; it may be completely insignificant to her, or she may not want to remember or talk about him. Are you prepared for that? Your birth parents may remember everything about your earliest days, yet withhold information about you, your origins, or each other. They may refuse to talk to you at all. They may not ever respond to you, except to deny that they are your biological parents. Can you imagine what that would feel like? Are you sure you want to risk finding out?

Even if your search is successful, reunion may be painful. Some adoptees tell me that their birth parents play cruel psychological cat-and-mouse games with them, that their birth parents are narcissistic, codependent, passive-aggressive, histrionic, obsessive, needy, or punitive. Some are weak, some are bullies, some are insecure, and some are abusive. None of these dysfunctions are unique to birth parents or to the relationship you have with them. You can find the same spectrum of personalities at school, work, your neighborhood, and the larger community. What's unique is that you may be willing to tolerate more dysfunction in the interest of connecting with your roots. Some adoptees find they will stay in a more toxic relationship with their birth parents than they would with anyone else, because the drive to connect is so strong. You have to know your own boundaries. I want you always to treat your birth parents with respect, but also take good care of yourself.

On the other hand, your search may go very well. Your birth parents may be perfectly wonderful people who are delighted you found them and eager to meet you. They may want to meet me, too. They may be healthy and happy. They may have fulfilling careers, close families, and lots of wonderful friends. Your birth mother may be regarded as an expert in her field. Your birth father may be the picture of life well-lived. I hope so.

Some adoptees tell me that their birth parents are simply lovely, that their birth parents are warm, nurturing, supportive, honest, open, and balanced. Some are interested, inclusive, encouraging, and affirming about reunion. Your birth parents might surpass your expectations; they may seem too good to be true, and initially, you may be happy that you searched, convinced that finding them was well worth everything you went through. You may feel completely at ease with each other and see no reason not to venture into a casual relationship. That would be great. Even so, I will encourage you to move slowly. I will ask you to consider the possibility that those feelings may change over time. One adoptee explained it to me this way:

> "For a while, after I reunited with my birth parents, we had a storybook relationship. They were wonderful people and we really hit it off. We started spending more and more time together, but the more time I spent with them, the more I began to resent them. They seemed so perfect, and I started to question why they adopted me out if they were as great as they seemed. I reverted back to my old thinking of there must be something wrong with *me*. When I tried to talk to them about it, all they would say was they weren't ready to be parents, which seemed selfish to me. They created me and then decided they didn't want to do it anymore? It seemed like they didn't have a big reason ... like they just didn't want to do it.

94

I felt like they made a huge decision about my life and they were just casual about it. It made me see them in a whole different light. I ended up breaking off contact, and I haven't seen them since. That was almost two years ago."

It's worth thinking about. If your birth parents seem to have their act together, why didn't they raise you? Why did they think I could do a better job? If they're really as loving and evolved as they seem to be, why couldn't they handle it? Why couldn't they handle *you*? It doesn't make sense. Unless ... hmm ... unless it *was* something about you. Unless you were "not right" in some vital, fundamental way.

Of course it wasn't anything about you! If you think it might have been, read this book twice. Then read it again! Your birth parents might seem to be nearly perfect people living a nearly perfect life, and you need to be clear in your own mind that their decision to make an adoption plan was about them, not you. It was a decision you may never fully understand. Instead of sizing up them and their lives as they are now, instead of making judgments about what they should or could have done differently, you need to believe to your bones that adoption was a decision they made after considering the circumstances of their lives at the time you were born. You need to believe it was the right decision for them to make. Otherwise, you're potentially setting yourself up for unnecessary personal pain, and no one needs more of that.

Have you thought about what you're going to do if you find that your birth records are permanently, legally, irrevocably closed? You may spend a lot of time and money searching without learning anything new. It would be easy for you to feel angry about that. It would be easy to resent your birth parents' secrecy. I know many adoptees who are downright bitter at their birth parents for that very thing, and some who seem to be bitter at everyone about everything. Issues of openness in adoption, original birth certificates, and adoptee rights have been publicized and debated and co-opted and politicized, and they will be again (maybe by you or me). But whether or not it's sociopolitically correct, and whether or not it's convenient or comfortable for you (or me), and whether or not you hang with a gang from Bastard Nation, your birth parents had a right to make the decisions they made as your first parents. They had a right to the full limits of privacy at the time, and they have that same right today. You owe it to them and yourself to accept that before you start a search.

I think you need to consider these possible outcomes of your search:

> Your birth parents may not want to see you or talk to you.
>
> They may tell you the pregnancy or the adoption plan was a terrible mistake.
>
> They may insist that you were taken from them against their wishes.
>
> They may lie about me or deny something you know is true.
>
> Your birth parents might want to see you once or twice and then refuse any further contact.
>
> They may be deceased.
>
> They may be mentally ill, in jail, or completely indifferent to you.
>
> Your birth mother and birth father may tell very different accounts about the circumstances leading up to your conception, your birth, your adoption, and the time since. They may each paint the other as villain and themselves as victim.

Your birth parents may resent me. They may resent you for being happy with me.

They may accuse you of being disloyal for taking your rightful place in our family.

They may threaten you.

They may share things that are painful for you to hear.

Your birth parents may want to take an active role in your life.

They may want to include you in their holiday celebrations and special events.

They may want you to include them in ours.

They may want you to leave your family and return to them.

They may think you owe them something.

They may want to advise you on important decisions or want you to advise them.

They may give you disturbing news about your genetic medical history.

You may not like them at all.

Are you ready for all those possibilities? Have you deeply and prayerfully considered how you would feel, what you would do, and how your life would change if any of that happened? If not, my child, I hope you'll postpone your search or reunion. You may lose a lot for very little gain. I know some adoptees who reunited with one or both birth parents and enjoy a positive relationship today. I also know many adoptees who didn't find what they were looking for or honestly wish they hadn't found their birth parents. Some adoptees find that reunion creates as many issues as it resolved. Their attempts to reestablish a bond ultimately fail, because the adoptees and their birth parents aren't able to get on the same page about the past, the present, *or* the future. One adoptee shared this with me:

> "I searched for my birth parents because I was curious. I wanted to see who I look like, and I wanted to hear from them why I was adopted. I met my birth mother and she was very nice, very warm, and friendly. She was much more outgoing than I am, but I liked her well enough. Right from the beginning, we struggled with each other's expectations. She looked at it like she had her daughter back and now it was time to make up for all the years we lost. She wanted my husband and me to be there for Sunday dinners and on the holidays. She wanted to be a part of my life … much more than I was ready for. I felt smothered and domineered, and I finally told her I wanted to take a break. I know it hurt her, but it was too much for me. I never got in touch with my biological father, even though I found contact information for him. That's enough for me right now."

Have you considered letting information be enough for you right now? Names … dates … medical history—might that be all you need? If you find out you got your high cheeks and olive skin from your birth mother and your fair hair and long fingers from your birth father, do you need to see the same on them? What if they had other children and decided to parent them? Your siblings … why them and not you? What if you discover that your birth mother never wanted you to be adopted away from her, that she was forced into it by her parents or a government policy? Do you want to imagine her daily anguish for the rest of your life, knowing that you can't do anything to help her heal? My child, I have a hard time understanding what that would add to your life.

There is something I'd like you to think about in case your reunion does go well. A meeting, however brief, will change all of you forever. You can't put a genie back in the bottle, and you won't be able to return your thoughts to your imaginary birth parents. Please, handle yourself and your birth parents with care. Respect them enough to be very clear about your expectations. If you agree to be in each other's lives, talk openly about what that means to each of you. Who decides how far "in"? Who decides how often you see each other, and is there an "out" clause if someone changes his or her mind? Never forget that your birth parents are real people with real feelings—people you will likely feel some obligation to, if not now, then after you search, find, and reunite with them. It's one thing to work it out as a fantasy, but the pain potential is much higher when you're dealing with real people who are as complex and fragile as anyone.

Are you prepared to know the circumstances in which your birth parents live? They may accept certain things as facts of life that you find intolerable, even immoral. Norms and customs vary so widely within and among countries, and you may be upset by some of the things you see and hear about. How will you feel if you find your birth siblings living without adequate supervision? What if your birth mother prostitutes herself in order to get by? Conversely, your birth parents may enjoy a higher standard of living than we do. They may have more money, a bigger home, better "stuff," and go on more fabulous vacations. How is that going to feel?

You need to be clear about the role you want your birth mother to play in your life. Are you inviting her in as a friend, a mentor, a babysitter, or a business partner? Can she call you on a whim about a great garage sale? Will you mind if she pops in at home or work? Does she have an open invitation to watch your concerts or games? She might expect you to spend some time with her on Mother's Day. After all, she made the ultimate sacrifice so you could have a better life. Is it too much to ask (she might say) that you would want to see her on Mother's Day? What if she wants to be Grandma to your kids? Is it all right with you if she introduces them to the religion or culture or language you left behind? How does your spouse feel about that?

You also need to be clear about the role you want your birth father to play in your life. Are you hoping he will offer you a job, come to your wedding, be your labor coach, or just send a letter now and then? Do you want to grill him about why he walked out on your young pregnant birth mother? Will you believe him if he says he didn't know about you until now? What if he wants to continue a relationship but you don't?

Your reunion (if it does happen) will be an event. Like your adoption, it will be significant, but still just an event. Your life, on the other hand, is a journey. Whatever the outcome of your search, your life will stretch before you as it does right now. No matter how it goes, I'll still be here, loving you as much as I do right now. You will still be my child. You will still be part of our family. We will still belong together. You will still have the life you've lived and the bonds you've created. None of that will ever go away. An adoptee and her birth mother said this to me:

> "I thank God every day that I found my first mother. It's hard to describe what it feels like to look in her eyes and know that she never stopped loving me. When people don't understand my relationship with her, I tell them, 'She's like a very special friend who I used to know but lost touch with. She knows things about me no one else knows, but she also accepts the person I am as an adult.'"

"Finding my daughter was one of the best things that ever happened to me. All I had were memories of her as a baby, and now I get to see how she's grown up. I'm grateful to her adoptive parents for being open to me. I don't want to take over. I just want to be able to love my daughter and know she's happy."

There's one more thing I need to say. The truth, my child, is that the outcome of your search makes no difference whatsoever. I want to be clear that I'm not minimizing the experience of search and reunion, or the feelings you may feel as part of your process. What I mean is that your birth story is merely an account of where you began. It isn't who you are. It isn't who you may become. The truth is that your birth story, whether exotic or plain, has no real bearing on the opportunity you have to create the life you want. For although you came from them, you are much more than whose body you came from, and they are much more than who they gave birth to. They merely started your life; you are living it. The ultimate truth is that you are you and they are they. You will always be You.

I Years Had Been from Home

I years had been from home,
And now, before the door,
I dared not open, lest a face
I never saw before

Stare vacant into mine
And ask my business there.
My business,—just a life I left,
Was such still dwelling there?

I fumbled at my nerve,
I scanned the windows near;
The silence like an ocean rolled,
And broke against my ear.

I laughed a wooden laugh
That I could fear a door,
Who danger and the dead had faced,
But never quaked before.

I fitted to the latch
My hand, with trembling care,
Lest back the awful door should spring,
And leave me standing there.

I moved my fingers off
As cautiously as glass,
And held my ears, and like a thief
Fled gasping from the house.

Emily Dickinson

Chapter 10

I Will Always Love You

I love you. I will always love you. No matter what you do or say, no matter where you go, no matter what words or time or distance pass between us, I will always love you. I will not always love all of your friends. I will not always approve of your behavior. I will not always like your choices or the decisions you make. I will not always understand. But I will always love you.

The desire to please others is a powerful force and one of the strongest motivators in the child-parent relationship. Children naturally want to gain their parents' favor and receive their parents' love in return. Some children mistakenly understand parental love as something given in exchange for good behavior or achievement. It's not. It is *not*. This is one of the most important things I will ever say to you. I love you with no strings attached. You don't have to earn my love. You don't have to be a certain way or do certain things to fulfill some dream of mine. You are my dream, just as you are.

I know some adoptees who think they have to earn their place in the family or be "good enough" to justify having been adopted.

As very young children, they worry that if they misbehave, they may be "given back" to their birth parents. When they get older, they worry that their parents secretly wish they had gotten a different kid. Some of them never get past feeling like a second choice or a default for their adoptive parents. One of my closest adoptee friends says she has always felt that her adoptive parents were disappointed with her, and her brother, who was also adopted into the family, made it clear from an early age that he wanted nothing to do with her. I can't imagine how any parents could be so cruel, especially parents who made the choice to adopt.

Have you ever worried that I'll find out something about your birth parents or your genetic history that will change the way I feel about you? It won't happen. Have you wondered how far you'd have to push me from your life for me to finally give up on you? It can't happen. Do you imagine that certain behaviors would cross some imaginary line in my heart and make me stop loving you? No such thing.

As our lives unfold, there will be times when either of us feels lonely or afraid or angry. We may hurt each other without meaning to. We may even hurt each other intentionally. As awful as that is, it happens in all families, and in most other relationships, too. One of the things that being family means is there is room in our relationship for all of our feelings. Nothing and no one can push us so far apart that we can't find our way back together again. I will not support all of your decisions, and if I think you're making a bad choice, I'm going to tell you so. I will always hold you to your highest standard whether or not it's convenient or popular or comfortable. Because I love you.

At times you will exceed my expectations, and at times you will fall short, and I'm sure I'll do the same. As your parent, I will be proud of your achievement and crushed by your defeat. I will be inspired by your determination and frustrated by your defiance. I will by turns be captivated, aggravated, illuminated, and irritated by what you do, but no matter what, I will always love you. We are a family, and regardless of what you lash out with in anger or pain, I will always love you.

Neither of us can predict the evolution of your feelings about adoption, your birth family, yourself, or me, but I know that I want you to share as much with me as you need to. Nothing you say will make me stop loving you or make me love you less. Children have an innate drive to individuate from their parents, a need to establish themselves as whole and separate from their parents. This is healthy and normal, and I would be concerned about you if you didn't have that impulse. I want you to pursue your self-actualization without fear of moving too far apart. Some adoptees say they are so afraid of alienating their parents that they never really develop a sense of themselves as independent adults. It's almost as if they're afraid to strike out on their own for fear that they won't be able to find their way back, or if they do, they may not be welcomed back. Don't worry about that. I'm not going anywhere that you can't find. I fully expect you to rubber band in and out of my life (and our home) at different times in your life. That's what family is for. I trust you won't go so far away that you'll forget the way home. We found each other once; we can do it again.

Sometimes personal development looks better from a distance. Friends and coworkers, teachers and distant relatives may notice only your burgeoning maturity, never guessing what toll your emergent independence may take on our relationship. Reality is that we can't always separate in degrees. Sometimes we have to tear the fabric of a relationship in order to be able to adjust it for a better fit. Then, once reshaped and adjusted, we're able to mend it and make it feel right again. I understand that. I accept that. I realize this is your first time through this life as my child. It's my first time through as your parent. We're both going to make a lot of mistakes.

I don't know if I should presume that you struggle or will struggle with fears of abandonment. So many adoptees say they do. Then again, many don't. I don't want to borrow trouble, but

I don't want to overlook something potentially very painful for you. I need you to take the lead on letting me in on what you feel and when and why. Is that asking too much? I know it's often difficult to sort your feelings into conversational parcels, so don't worry about saying things exactly right, just tell me what's on your mind. I can't get into your head and pull your thoughts out, so I don't really know what you feel unless you tell me.

At some point you may question what you know of your birth parents and your adoption story. Ask me. I'll tell you. At some time you may feel unlovable. I hope not, but if you do, I hope you'll tell me. I can reassure you that everyone feels that way sometimes. I can remind you how much your birth mother loved you and how very much I love you now.

Love Is Anterior to Life

Love is anterior to life,
Posterior to death,
Initial of creation, and
The exponent of breath.

Emily Dickinson

Notes

Chapter 4
1. William Wordsworth, *The Rainbow*
2. Cohen, Joyce S,; Westhues, Anne, "A Comparison of Self-Esteem, School Achievement, and Friends between Intercountry Adoptees and Their Siblings," *Early Child Development and Care*, v106, p205-24, Feb 1995.
3. Search Institute Profiles of Student Life, 1999.

Chapter 6
1. Alfred A. Knopf, *Children First, What Our Society Must Do, And Is Not Doing, For Our Children Today,* Penelope *Leach* (NY: 1994), 33.
2. http://www.babyscoopera.com, accessed September 2009.

Made in the USA
Middletown, DE
02 January 2022

57486355R00070